WHAT A
SON
NEEDS
FROM HIS
MOM

WHAT A
S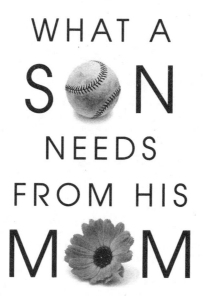N
NEEDS
FROM HIS
M⬤M

CHERI FULLER

BETHANY HOUSE PUBLISHERS

a division of Baker Publishing Group
Minneapolis, Minnesota

Published by Bethany House Publishers
11400 Hampshire Avenue South
Bloomington, Minnesota 55438
www.bethanyhouse.com

Bethany House Publishers is a division of
Baker Publishing Group, Grand Rapids, Michigan

Printed in the United States of America

Library of Congress Cataloging-in-Publication Data
Fuller, Cheri.
    What a son needs from his mom / Cheri Fuller.
        p. cm.
    Includes bibliographical references.
    Summary: "Presents advice for mothers on how to raise caring, confident young
men. Includes tips for boys' different ages. Topics include learning the balance between controlling and letting go, cultivating a boy's unique masculinity, and encouraging a lasting relationship with God"—Provided by publisher.
    ISBN 978-0-7642-1030-3 (pbk. : alk. paper)
    1. Mothers and sons. 2. Sons—Psychology. 3. Child rearing. 4. Mothers and
sons—Religious aspects—Christianity. I. Title.
HQ755.85.F853 2013
306.874'3—dc23   2012040441

Cover design by Lookout Design, Inc.

Author is represented by WordServe Literary Group

14   15   16   17   18   19   10 9 8 7

To
Justin Oliver Fuller
and
Christopher Kenton Fuller,

my sons, who've been a blessing to me
throughout their lives
and grown into wonderful, caring, confident men,
and the *best dads* I know.

Love you forever
and like you for always,

Mom

Contents

Contents

1

Mothers and Sons

There is an enduring tenderness in the love of a
mother to a son that transcends all other affections
of the heart.

—Washington Irving

One morning when our first son, Justin, was barely two, I walked
into the kitchen after putting his freshly washed jeans and T-
shirts in his chest of drawers and turned to the family room,
where he'd been playing just moments before.

He was gone.

"Justin!" I called as I looked around. *I just saw him playing
with his big dump truck. How could he disappear like that?*

"Justin! Justin! Where are you? Are you hiding? Where are
you, honey?" I searched all over the house, in every closet and
cranny, calling his name, looking under beds and behind doors,
thinking he was playing hide-and-seek.

Oh, he must have gone to the backyard. My heart raced as I ran outside, but no Justin. After searching the house one more time, I ran to the front door and found it unlocked. *How did he reach the lock?* I wondered as I charged outside, calling his name at the top of my lungs.

I didn't see anyone in the yard or in the street. But finally I looked up and saw our little blond, blue-eyed toddler sitting high on the roof above me, smiling and happy as he could be. That smile of conquest said it all: "I did it!"

Below him was a tall ladder some workmen had left leaning against our house when they went to lunch.

"Stay right there and I'll get you!" I yelled. Clearly, this pint-size boy wasn't nearly as scared as I was. "Mommy, it's okay," he called down, looking poised to explore even higher.

Though high places are not my thing, I climbed up the ladder, put my arm around my little boy, and carried him down to safety. This wasn't his last climbing adventure, and I found out later why he had a bent toward climbing. My mother-in-law told me she often found her firstborn son (my husband and Justin's dad) in the top of twenty-five-foot trees at the park even as a very young boy.

Justin continued to love high places and to be able to climb out of anything (his car seat, for one) and to the highest part of playground equipment. There were a few scary incidents ahead, like when he climbed to our top kitchen cabinets and ate several of my allergy pills just to see what they tasted like. After that, we got the even more secure child-safety locks and bought a tall geodesic dome for (safe) backyard climbing!

The rest of the story: In college, Justin began bouldering and rock climbing in the Colorado mountains and in climbing gyms, and has loved the sport ever since. He has passed down his passion for climbing to his daughter, Caitlin, who is a competitive rock climber and made it to the U.S. Nationals at the age of eleven. She's fifteen now, and sport climbing is her favorite athletic endeavor.

Justin's roof-climbing adventure was just one early point on the long learning curve called raising boys! Having grown up in the middle of five sisters and a much younger brother, boys were always a bit of a mystery to me. I didn't know much about boy-energy. I was raised in a girl-world of dolls and dancing lessons, tea parties, games, and cute ruffled dresses Mama made for us. When we did pretend play, we donned her high heels and put on her makeup, or pretended to be Florence Nightingale as we played "nurse."

My sons' costumes and pretend play couldn't have been more different. From a young age, Justin and Christopher's favorite costumes were cowboy and army wear, homemade Superman and Batman capes, and boys' hats of all kinds: fireman, worker man, army man—as they called them.

When we visited my mom on her ranch in east Texas, the boys got to don their cowboy gear and ride a pony, go fishing, and tramp around in the woods with their cousins. I learned early on that some boys had *adventure needs* I'd never thought of or experienced. Over and over as they grew, I saw that these precious boys were different from us females and had unique needs, behavior, communication styles, desires, and ways of processing things in the world around them.

Yet oh, how I love my boys! Through every year of their childhood, middle school, and adolescent years, and into adulthood, I've learned more and more about raising sons. Now Justin and Chris are grown men, parents themselves. And with three granddaughters and three grandsons, I'm still coming to a deeper understanding and enjoyment of the marvelous males around me.

Why a Son Needs His Mom

Maternal love is perhaps the most powerful, positive influence on a son's development and life. Don't let anybody convince you that you are irrelevant in your son's life or that you need to separate from him prematurely. If you are the only woman in an all-male family, it can seem like the boys and your husband are a tight group (especially if he is very involved in their lives). You may even think your sons don't need you. But nothing could be further from the truth!

Moms make an indelible imprint on the lives of their children. As Dr. William Pollack wrote in *Real Boys*, how mothers "respond to baby boys and young sons—the manner in which [they] cuddle, kiss, and reassure, teach, comfort, and love—not only determines a young boy's capacity for a healthy emotional start in life but deeply affects a boy's characteristic style of behavior and the development of his brain."[1]

If you are a single mother, or your son's dad is absent emotionally or physically, it can seem like a daunting task to raise a boy alone. But there are many great men who were raised by single moms: Alexander Haig, former U.S. Chief of Staff and Secretary of State; Ed Bradley, award-winning news correspondent; Dr. Benjamin Carson, acclaimed surgeon; Barack Obama, President of the United States; and Samuel Jackson, actor, to name a few.

As John and Helen Burns say in their book, *What Dads Need to Know About Daughters/What Moms Need to Know About Sons*:

> Unfortunately, sometimes the father role gets so overemphasized that mothers feel helpless and incapable of raising masculine boys without the help of a strong father figure. This notion is an oversimplification; many single mothers have raised stellar young men who are very masculine.[2]

The reality is there are *many* reasons a son needs his mom. In the early years, she provides safety, love, and nurture—or TLC (tender loving care)—gifts that are vital to his emotional security and even lifelong relationships. Yes, there are other people in a boy's life that influence him, like his father, grandparents, teachers, sisters, brothers, and coaches. Yet the first and strongest influence is his mother.

One of the greatest needs a son has in his first two years is a secure attachment and bond with his mom. According to researcher Elizabeth Carlson,

When a mother reacts reliably and sensitively to her infant's needs, he will form an internal connection to her—what psychologists call "a secure attachment"—that will provide a strong foundation of trust and love on which he can build other relationships.[3]

A boy needs his mother to make their house a safe, loving place to live. It's a gift to provide our sons a loving refuge and a warm meal, a chance to gather around the table for conversation, even with take-out pizza.

"Some of the most important things for a mother to do are simple and joyous," Daniel Hast told me. Reflecting on his childhood, the now thirty-two-year-old said,

Seldom do you meet someone who can both cook and bake— but my mom can. She can bake pies, cookies, cakes, all kinds of good things. Just as all mothers do, my mom made mistakes. But I'll take the memories, good fond memories of coming in from school and smelling some fabulous apple pie she was just getting out of the oven.

So many kids I knew got raised on frozen Eggo waffles, so it conveyed love to me that Mom made things from scratch. Little details like that make for a joyous upbringing. There's something to be said for homemade apple pie, chocolate chip cookies, snickerdoodles, gingersnaps, candied spiced pecans—simple things that make good memories and bring happiness.

No Perfect Moms

I want you to know that I don't approach the sacred subject of raising children as if there is some magic formula or pretend that we can do parenting in a perfect way. The truth is that the perfect mom/perfect child concept is a myth. The only perfect parent is God, and look at the trouble He had with His kids, Adam and Eve. If we aim for perfection, and expect the result of our earnest efforts or parenting formula to be perfect Christian children, we may be very disappointed—not only in ourselves, but in our child and in God.

There is no perfect family, mom, dad, or kids! Parenting is both a challenge and a privilege—whether biological mom or adoptive mom. God doesn't promise an easy ride, but He promises to *always* be with us. You can depend on the Lord's infinite grace to nurture and love your child—because He chose you of all the women in the world to be his mother.

Instead of simple recipes for raising the ideal son, this book offers my experiences and those of other moms, as well as suggestions and insights that I hope will help you understand your son's needs better at different stages in his life. That's a first step to meeting his needs and staying connected.

Being a Mother of Boys

The nineteenth-century nursery rhyme[4] describes boys as all about "snips and snails and puppy dogs tails," and it is true, some little guys *are* fascinated with frogs, slimy slugs, and creepy-crawly creatures.

Boys often like to run, climb, make messes, and occasionally push the envelope on the rules. That's why parenting them is such an adventure—sometimes loud and often active. But there are plenty of boys whose passion is playing piano, singing, or dance; other boys who love to take apart toasters and lawn mowers; and some who will sit and quietly build with Legos, play video games, or be on the computer for hours.

There are many joys in raising boys. "Raising three sons was heaven on earth," said Lisa, a Dallas mother. "My boys were always ready to go outside and have fun. They loved adventures, camping, and fishing, and I do, too! They forgave easily and let things roll off their backs. Teenage sons—that was more stressful. But I've always loved their affection for me."

Michelle Garrett of Edmond, Oklahoma, said, "My three boys can make me laugh, they can frustrate me, they sometimes scare me to death, and at other times can make me feel like the best mama around."

Even though we love our boys so much we'd throw ourselves in front of a bus to save them, many of us have also found raising sons to be a long learning curve filled with joy *and* challenges. One of those is the mixed message we face: Our hearts tell us to hold our sons close and give them lots of love and affection, but the culture around us says that can create "Mama's boys" who won't be able to make it in the real world.

Another confusing aspect of parenting sons is how different they are from girls—right from the start! One mom told me, "After three daughters I hardly knew what to do when my baby boy's pee flew in my face the first time I changed his diaper. Even as a toddler, he's all boy, obsessed with trucks, jets, and army men."

I had and still have no interest in guns, as many moms have expressed. Although I didn't buy our firstborn play guns, before long he was making them out of sticks and even bananas. I eventually accepted this and let him do his good guy/bad guy action play.

Carol, a mother of a son and a daughter, described raising her son as daunting:

> As a mom, you're in charge of raising a human being who acts and thinks and looks *exactly the opposite* of you—in every way there is. You may feel under-qualified from the beginning because you're the opposite sex. I did! You have to prepare yourself for the fact that you're raising a human being who is different from you. It's interesting how boys and girls work and think. I can reason with my daughter because we think alike as females; we track with each other. With our son, I have to approach reasoning and communicating with him in a totally different way.

The theme of *learning* and *challenge* pops up frequently in my conversations with mothers. Raising a boy can even bring us to our knees. "My son was a challenge from the get-go. He challenged every rule, decision, and authority," says Janet, a San Antonio mom. She continues:

> Because of this, I had to learn how to pray. God knew that this child would need a praying mother, and I knew that I desperately needed a God who was and is almighty! I should have named my son Salmon because he was always swimming upstream. Yet he needed that constitution and strength when as a young adult he stepped out in faith to follow God as a pastor and church planter.

What Will You Find in This Book?

To grow into healthy, caring, confident men, boys need their moms. But part of the delicate balance we must understand and apply is what our son needs at different stages of development. That helps us find the balance between closeness and distance, giving him a strong foundation and yet developing his wings so he can take off someday.

A mother's love doesn't make her son more dependent and timid; it actually makes him stronger and more independent. To borrow William Pollack's words, your love is "tremendously valuable, and it truly helps boys become confident, powerful, successful men."[5] The place of safety a loving, stable mom provides gives boys the courage to explore and grow. So we'll look at the encouragement, safety, support, comfort, and trust boys gain from their mothers.

I have also included chapters to help you understand your son's unique personality and learning patterns. As you read, you'll learn about the needs of a boy and how those needs change from childhood to adolescence.

> Understanding is the beginning of positive influence. A mother's desire to understand her son can equip her with the power to influence his life for good, thereby influencing his family, and his family's family, and all the generations to come.[6]

In addition, you will discover ways to listen and encourage your son, to help him become a confident decision maker, and help him deal with his emotions. We'll look at how moms can build strong character in their sons and how to unlock their potential in school. You'll also find some keys to finding a balance between staying connected but not hovering and controlling as your son grows.

We will also look at ways to cover your sons' lives with prayer. And last, how to take care of ourselves so that we can better parent now as well as when it's time to release them to manhood in a way that their energy isn't drained by worrying about us.

I've interviewed many mothers in different seasons of life who have raised or are raising boys of all ages, and you'll read some of their stories as well as my own. I have also collected thoughts and feedback from guys young and old. By listening to these sons' voices, we will understand their needs more clearly.

As we begin, I want to assure you I certainly wasn't the perfect mom to our sons nor was our experience entirely smooth and problem free. Yet I have learned so much in my years of raising our sons, Justin and Chris. They are truly amazing men, husbands, and fathers we are extremely grateful for and proud of. I'm also excited to share with you what I have learned through being a grandma to three preteen grandsons.

Along the way, you'll find questions in each chapter for you to think about or discuss with your girlfriends, small group, or mom's group.

Whether you have a baby boy or a preschooler, an elementary- or middle-school-age boy, or your son has charged into adolescence or college and career, I'm glad you have joined me and other moms on this journey.

Questions to Ponder, Journal, or Discuss

1. What has been your experience so far with mothering sons? How would you describe what it's like to raise a boy?

2. What is one of your son's needs that you have found ways to meet?

3. What have been your biggest challenges so far in mothering your son?

4. What differences from you (or your daughters or sisters) do you see in your son—physically, mentally, or emotionally? How do you respond to these?

5. What do you have the most anxiety about in raising a boy?

2

A Mom Who Encourages

Gentle words are a tree of life.

—Proverbs 15:4 NLT

Our neighbor Evan, a six-foot-tall high school soccer player, and I were talking one day in the front yard about a car accident he'd just had. "My mom is my greatest encourager," he told me. "I talk to my dad about sports a lot, but when I really need encouragement, it's my mom I go to."

After the wreck, he told his mom how sorry he was and how bad he felt about damaging the car. Evan told me if she had said negative things like, "Why weren't you being smarter?" or "I told you so," it would have brought him down more because he already felt horrible about the accident. Instead, she told Evan there were so many worse things that could have happened. She agreed it was his fault, but instead of piling on more guilt, she was just glad he was safe.

Evan's mom is also an encourager when his team loses or he doesn't perform well. She highlights a positive thing he did instead of wrong moves or kicks he missed in the match. Her encouragement also extends beyond sports, Evan said.

> Although most of my friends and high school classmates drink and smoke, I don't. I'd be so much more stressed if my mom was negative, and there'd be much more of a temptation. Whether it's about girls, soccer, problems, or my academics, she's always open to talking with me about things that matter. I know I can always go to her to discuss things and leave encouraged.

Every day we have the opportunity to either encourage our sons or discourage them. The natural tendency is to point out things they are doing wrong. Although said with good intentions to bring improvement or motivate, the opposite results. A continual barrage of critical words only discourages a boy's motivation and derails the loving relationship we hope to build.

Why? Because people, especially children and teens, tend to recoil from those who criticize them. They move toward those who encourage them and away from those who discourage them.

Throughout the years of raising Justin and Christopher, I found it helped to "focus on the donut instead of the hole" when we talked. For example, focusing on the donut means highlighting your son's efforts in a game rather than whether their team won or lost. It means blessing him with praise for making progress instead of pointing out deficiencies (the hole). If your son shows you his artwork, avoid saying, "That's really good, but you know you could do better." It produces great frustration, especially in younger kids.

This kind of negative approach focuses on the "hole"—what our sons are not doing well or how they're falling short. Without our realizing it, our negative, critical words deflate rather than lift up and inspire.

Praising Kids

Across the board, research shows that when kids are praised for their intelligence and told how smart they are ("You made an A+ without studying. You're a genius!"), they avoid risks in order to keep looking smart. Parents with good intentions are trying to build their kids' self-esteem. But making them feel smarter doesn't help them fulfill their potential. Kids often show a drop in effort and interest in what they're learning and are more inclined to lie about their scores so they can keep up the appearance of being "smart." When these students run into harder problems, they assume *I must not be good at this* and stop trying. Just what we don't want our sons to do—give up!

However, studies show that when students are praised for their effort ("You got eight right; you must have worked very hard for that score"), they are actually energized by difficult questions. When they face a challenging task, they think it means they should try harder and are motivated to learn new things. In a key study, effort-praised students saw significant improvement at school, made the best scores, and were less likely to lie about their marks.[1]

You can apply this effort-praising principle to your son by saying things like "You worked hard and finished your book report even though it was a 200-page book. I like that," or "Good work going after the science fair prize," or "I appreciate how you stuck in there, playing your hardest all season even though your team was in last place." Letting boys know that *effort and hard work is a key ingredient* in all pursuits in life is an important message.

Boys need to know that ordinary kids who put forth extraordinary effort can accomplish great things. That helps them meet challenges head-on and be willing to double their efforts when they reach more difficult work. Helping your son see that mistakes give him helpful information to learn from, and that he is *not dumb* when he does make a mistake, will give him courage to persevere.

We also need to encourage our sons' dreams. Daniel told me how his mother encouraged him and his brother: "When I'd said, 'I want to grow up to be an astronaut, fighter pilot, etc.' she didn't respond, 'Oh, that's crazy.' She was always very supportive of us and our dreams."

Encouraging words may seem small and even inconsequential, but they plant seeds of good character, promise, and blessing in your son's life.

While preschool boys need buckets of encouragement, that need changes when they get to elementary school, where the need for *achievement* is key. At that stage, they need to start knowing what they are good at and not good at. Later in this chapter I'll talk more about how to encourage older boys, but for now, know to praise generously where it's real and give realistic feedback in areas of weakness.[2]

Unconditional Love: "Just Because You're You"

A few years ago my daughter, Ali, started saying to her boys before bed, "You're doing such a great job of being five" (or whatever age they were). She did this both for the boys' sake, to affirm and allow them to be who they were right then, and for her sake as their mother, to stay focused on the present, to worry less about what they weren't doing, and to focus on what they *were doing incredibly well*—being who they were for the age they were. In these nightly, loving words, the boys felt accepted not for performance but for being the little guys they were at the time.

During Noah's tenth year, Ali began to see the impact of her words. "It really makes a difference," she told me. "I've had some special moments with Noah in a very pivotal year. He's getting more independent and he's thinking more on his own. It feels different and I could take offense, but when I tell him he's doing such a great job of being ten, it refocuses my energy on encouraging and affirming his process of growth instead of grieving that he's getting older or taking his growing independence the wrong way."

This practice of simple encouragement also happens at bedtime, when the boys hug their mom and might feel open enough to talk about some things with her.

> I'm learning boys put a lot of pressure on themselves that we as moms don't realize. How quickly we can multiply their feelings of not measuring up by saying something like "be respectful" over and over. For Noah, that's interpreted that he's not being respectful to people; yet he really wants to be even when he occasionally has human moments that we all do.[3]

Another way to encourage boys of elementary- and middle-school age is to share stories of athletes and others who overcame major obstacles to achieve their dreams. Rarely were the Olympic athletes winners at age five or six; their parents weren't stunned by their latent ability. Often they struggled with health issues or school problems, were told they couldn't compete, or faced other obstacles.

Many professional athletes have triumphed after cancer or disease: Jim Abbott was born without a right hand, yet went on to pitch in the Major Leagues and even threw a no-hitter for the New York Yankees. Red Sox third baseman Mike Lowell, Olympic swimmer Eric Shanteau, Olympic gold medal figure skater Scott Hamilton, and NFL punter Josh Bidwell are other role models whose stories are valuable to share with your son because they show it's not just about ability. It's not just what you're naturally good at. Achieving anything worthwhile is really about hard work and determination, triumphing over adversities, working toward a goal, and not giving up.

It's important to celebrate and praise our boys who are gifted in ways beyond athletic or physical pursuits: those who are inventive, creative, and innovative thinkers, poets, and tinkerers. In *Raising Cain*, child psychologists Dan Kindlon and Michael Thompson advise,

> We need to teach boys that there are many ways to become a man; that there are many ways to be brave, to be a good father, to be loving and strong and successful. . . . We need to praise the artist and the entertainer, the missionary and the athlete, the soldier and the male nurse, the store owner and the round-the-world sailor, the teacher and the CEO. There are many ways to make a contribution in this life.[4]

Encouraging Adolescent Boys

For boys ages thirteen forward, it's a little more challenging to encourage them because they have an increasing need for *autonomy*. Most teenagers don't like being helped, told what to do, or sometimes even encouraged by their mothers. Adolescent boys have days when they are prickly or out of sorts. In their perspective, our words can sound like a "knower" (Mom) informing the "one who doesn't know" (her son). Sometimes even your loving statements may be rejected because they don't like the sound of being told who or what they are, even if it's positive or encouraging.

Ken Wilgus, a Dallas psychologist who has counseled hundreds of adolescents and parents, told me he usually advises parents of teenagers to make their encouraging statements in "smaller" terms. Ken said making an encouragement smaller is done two ways: First, comment on specific events or actions, not global characterizations (e.g., "It really helps me when you're on time and ready like this"). And second, personalize the comment. It's easier for a teenage boy to swallow "I don't know about anyone else, but *to me* you seemed to give it your all through the whole football game," rather than something like "You were the best one on the field! You're going to be an NFL player someday."

Third, be real and genuine. Don't slather on excessive praise or be grandiose. That creates praise junkies who depend on other people's affirmation and praise to keep going. Mike, a twenty-something coach, told me,

> I needed honest words of encouragement from my mother, especially when I was a teenager, but what I got were obligatory comments like a checklist: "How was practice? I'm sure you did awesome," with no eye contact, no listening to my answer. In fact, I'd done a poor job that day and I knew I wasn't awesome. She also used too many words. She hounded me too much about practice, homework, games, whatever, so I tuned her out. What a son needs most from his mom is physical and verbal affirmation. But most of all for her to be real and honest.

And if your son has a bad game and you both know it, don't tell him you're so proud of him. "Don't be a mother who always says, 'Good job,' if he didn't do a good job . . . because he's going to see straight through that," said one young man. "Just say, 'Hey, I'm sorry you guys lost, but I noticed you never gave up,' or 'You know, today wasn't your day . . . you're not going to win every game.' That helps them learn to deal with failure, which every boy and man needs to do."

Two simple words—"I noticed"—can also infuse encouragement in a subtle way: "I noticed you got everything done for your science project without any help." "I noticed you've been setting out your clothes and athletic stuff the night before. Good organization." "I noticed how kind you were to your sister."

A Picture Is Worth 1,000 Words

There is another way to encourage sons that doesn't use spoken words. Alison grew up with two older brothers, and when she had two sons of her own, she realized that being around boys all her life gave her a priceless education: Words often fail with boys, especially in medium to large doses. For example, from the first day of kindergarten to the last day of third and fourth grades, her boys would jump in the car after a long school day with one thing on their minds—*food*. The last thing on their mind: *talking*. She learned early that questions were not welcome until food was nestled nicely in their stomachs.

One day she stumbled upon a set of pictures with short quotes. When she read the hopeful stories behind the pictures on a website, she was amazed by the amount of encouragement they offered to buoy a person through life's challenges. At the time she was in the throes of postpartum depression and didn't know how she was going to encourage her precious little boys to be all they were created to be when she was so terribly down herself.

When the posters arrived in the mail, she tacked them up in her sons' rooms, in the living room, and in the hallway. For almost a decade now the boys have walked by the visible yet not imposing photographs: someone overcoming an obstacle, an ordinary person achieving something extraordinary. Posters mounted on walls in a house have spoken a thousand words, making her goal of encouraging her sons more doable and the need to lecture nearly obsolete. And day by day, with each glance they take, courage and hope are strengthened in the boys' hearts.

One of the most impacting posters reads "Team Hoyt," and under it is a photograph of a father pushing his adult son in a specially designed wheelchair across a finish line. She told her boys the story about the Hoyts, how she saw them run the Oklahoma Memorial Marathon years before and the indelible impact of the father's devotion—pushing his son not only through that race but over 1,000 marathons and triathlons. This and other stories are now wedged in their memories, reinforced through the visual reminders. As Noah and Luke, now ten and eleven, have grown in understanding about what devotion means, as well as overcoming adversity and working together, they have begun to internalize these values.

"I find as the boys get older, words and long-winded attempts at encouraging them to press on during challenging moments— whether encountering a bully at school or giving 110 percent in soccer practice in the summer heat—roll off their backs," Alison told me. "I can see their eyes glaze over if I reach maximum word capacity for what they're able to ingest at one time. It's like an involuntary eye roll creeps into our conversation!"

Instead of taking it personally, she's adapted a way of encouraging the boys along their unique and constantly changing paths. She paints short quotes with art borders and frames them to encourage the boys when they are facing something new or challenging. They speak more than mere words can express.

This mom doesn't know if she's impacting her sons the way she hopes by pasting paper to walls and chalkboard paint. But she sees her boys' eyes land on them occasionally, watches as they pause for a quick read, a quiet *hmmm*, or a simple head tilt before blazing out the door to shoot hoops. Sometimes they say, "Hey, good one, Mom" when they see a new quote posted on the whiteboard. And every once in a while she even gets the thrill of walking into a room surprised to find a boy's handwritten treasure of his own, like "'Every wall is a door.' —Ralph Waldo Emerson," which Luke had posted on his bedroom wall recently.

A Man's Need for Encouragement

As our boys grow into young men and adults, they don't outgrow their basic need for support. You might get some eye rolling, or your son might not tell you he needs encouraging words, but do it anyway. Even when our sons move across the country or have their own families, we can still be a source of encouragement.

Studies demonstrate this need. After two years of extensive research with hundreds of men, Patrick Morley discovered that men's second greatest need, besides companionship, is for *support*. They described this need with words such as *more understanding, encouragement, appreciation, respect, affirmation, acceptance, significance, purpose, fulfillment*. It sounds like what they're saying is "Help me out here . . . I need some encouragement!"[5]

Whether it's on their birthdays, Father's Day, or other occasions, I like to encourage our adult sons by writing a short note in a card, such as "I respect you for the devoted father and husband you are" or "I love how you put your family first and take care of them so well." I write how much I admire a recent accomplishment or tell them what a blessing they are to me.

On Mother's Day I've sent them cards saying, "I'm so thankful I've gotten to be your mom!"

Interestingly, Justin, our oldest, told me recently he's soaked in more of this encouragement as a grown-up:

> Mom, I remember seasons where you were real encouraging about school in areas where I struggled like math or Spanish, or struggled with comparing myself with Chris's performance. It's been a lifelong habit of yours to encourage all three of your children.
>
> But your encouragement in my adult years is easier for me to remember in a way. I appreciate your words more because it's hard to internalize much as a teenager; it rolls off your back. Your words have stuck more and felt more real because you have a perspective on my role as a father, husband, and provider, be-cause you're talking with me and encouraging me, adult to adult.
>
> Calling out positives is what you do. It doesn't have to be something big, with serious overtones, or especially profound. It can be as simple as calling out a specific quality. That's what your encouragement always sounds like to me: calling out positives. Reminding me that I'm capable, or working hard, that I'm lov-ing my kids well, that you're proud of who I am. It means a lot.

"I Believe in You"

Although they need affirmation that we believe in them, en-couraging our adult sons can be like walking a fine line. It takes wisdom *not* to tell them what they should do but support them while they're trying to figure it out—especially when they seem to be floundering or frustrated.

When Alice's adult son's job ended, he told her he wanted to look for a new, more fulfilling line of work. The trouble was he didn't know what kind of work that would be and now he was unemployed. He'd never been interested in climbing the corporate ladder and doesn't define success in annual income. He just made broad statements like "I want to do something that will benefit other people."

Alice recognized that as a young adult of thirty-one, her son was grappling with his own significance—looking for a way to make a difference in the world. Several weeks went by and he became discouraged at his inability to determine what kind of work would meet his need for income and his desire to contribute to people.

Rather than offering advice, Alice asked questions, such as, "If money were no object, what would you do with your time?" and "What do you care most about?" As he wrestled with the answers, she assured him that she knew he'd figure it out, that she believed in him and knew he had a lot to offer.

A few more weeks went by as her son explored his options. Then one day he announced that he had enrolled in a nutritional coaching school and taken a job at a local health food store. Her Mama heart rejoiced at the news, especially when he smiled and said, "Mom, thanks for your encouragement and for giving me the space to find my way. I don't know what I would have done without your coaching."

Let me encourage you not to wait to offer kind words until your sons are older, more successful, make top grades, or behave better. Avoid taking it personally if your encouraging words aren't appreciated. And don't let a critical spirit cloud or damage your relationship with your son. It's tempting, especially if you're a perfectionist or have super-high expectations of his performance, or you wait until he's done something spectacular to comment on it. Focus on the hidden gifts you see within him that may not be in bloom yet and accept your son right where he is. Be full of grace and enjoy being your son's cheerleader in the race of life. I've found by personal experience that a mother's genuine words of encouragement are very powerful and have far-reaching effects.

Even in the toddler days, I never saw our sons—or daughter, for that matter—as just sniffly, messy, silly kids. From an early age, I saw them as the young people and then adults they were going to be someday. This helped me value and respect our children and thus encourage them as individuals with God-given gifts and strengths, full of potential, no matter what the obstacles might be ahead of them. I'm so grateful to be their mom!

Questions to Ponder, Journal, or Discuss

1. How does your son best hear and receive encouraging words from you?

2. When is a time you felt rejected or not listened to when you were trying to support or affirm him?

3. What did you learn from this chapter that you could apply to your parenting right now?

4. What builds your son's sense of self-worth?

5. Considering how to "focus on the donut instead of the hole," what consists of your son's "donut"—what he's giving effort toward, his skills or strengths, something he's made progress in?

3

A Mom Who Builds Confidence in Her Son

Courage is not simply one of the virtues but the form
of every virtue at the testing point, which means at
the point of highest reality.

—C. S. Lewis

One day as my husband, Holmes, and I were looking at old
photos a month after his mom died, he reminisced about his
adventures growing up in Pawhuska, a small town in northern
rural Oklahoma.

"She was always three steps ahead, preparing me for future
things I didn't even know about," Holmes said. "Like when I
was eight years old, Mom gave me books about courage, character, patriotism, adventure, and overcoming adversity—and
encouraged me to read them." Joan, or Mimi as we called her,
realized Holmes liked history instead of science fiction, so she
gave him books about the Revolutionary and Civil Wars and

biographies of great men like those in *Profiles in Courage* and *General Douglas MacArthur,* which he read over and over. That's where he began to develop a lifelong love of history, and decades later he is still enjoying reading great works of history.

When he was fourteen, Mimi encouraged Holmes to get Red Cross and CPR training so he'd have the opportunity someday to be a swimming instructor and lifeguard. That paved the way for him to have a good job at the town's country club during high school and college summers and teach scores of kids how to swim and dive. He taught swimming all day and then did a shift at the local hospital.

She also gave Holmes a lot of freedom. From third grade on, he rode his horse around their land. After school and on weekends, he rode for miles and miles. Never fearful or controlling, she let him make his own decisions with some gentle guidance. For example, when as a seven-year-old he wanted to climb in the rocky hills and woods alone or with a friend, she advised him where to look for snakes. What a brave mother! All his adventures helped Holmes become more self-reliant, courageous, and skilled at problem solving, which built a sense of confidence at a young age.

Not all of us can raise our sons in a rural area where it's more possible to provide freedom to explore, but we can foster competency and build their confidence wherever we live. For boys dream of adventure—"fighting bad guys, exploring, uncovering hidden treasure . . . there are mountains to climb, rivers to ford."[1] We can nurture the confidence to pursue their God-given desires. That's what this chapter is about.

You may be wondering whether confidence is inborn or learned. When I taught school, there were students who walked into my classroom with a natural sense of confidence. Others were more tentative and self-doubting by nature and grew more confident as they developed skills and areas of strength. But while a sense of confidence (believing he is capable but without arrogance) develops on the inside of a boy, it is strongly influenced by his relationships and especially how he is treated by his parents.

When they are young, kids measure their worth on how they are valued and perceived by others, especially Mom and Dad. So our love, acceptance, and confidence in our sons—which includes having faith in and believing in their abilities—is an important building block. So is the competency they gain when they become good at doing something, which helps self-worth and assurance grow. Step by step as confidence grows, boys develop courage. They begin to make choices and take action without being paralyzed by fear of failure.

As you read this chapter, if you are having a sinking feeling that your son is distinctly tentative and anything but confident, please read on. It's not too late to help him develop confidence!

Raising Confident Boys: First Things First

The major way a mother can foster confidence in her son in the preschool years is to build his sense of security by warm, responsive care, hugging, approval, structure, buckets of love, and encouragement. I love what educator Jane Healy said: "The brain of a child who feels secure, loved, and happy can direct all its attention toward learning and growth rather than focusing on worries and fears."[2]

Because emotional development is the centerpiece of children's learning and growth, the infant and toddler years are the prime time for emotional nurturing. All the cuddling, feeding, and nurturing it takes to meet your baby's needs in the first few years is a great investment. With it, you and your son can develop a loving, trusting bond, and he develops emotional security. The early bond provides the foundation for his ability to learn, develop self-control and empathy, his capacity to communicate, cooperate, and relate to others for a lifetime.

In the preschool and elementary years, boys need big chunks of their mom's time to fill up their emotional tank. This inner tank isn't filled by elaborate electronic toys, Mozart CDs (although classical music is great), or high-definition TV and screen time.

Their emotional tank is filled when we take time to scoop our little boy up on our lap and read a book to him, sit on the floor and build blocks with him, or play catch or board games together. By sitting by his bed after lights out to listen, pray a prayer of blessing, and give a back rub, it provides another opportunity to be together. All of this builds a sense of security in our young son.

Most moms are good at this part of parenting! As we will look at later in this chapter, the more challenging time comes in adolescence.

Young boys need to have room, time, and opportunities to explore and not be cooped up inside. Ruthie Hast, therapist and mother of two grown sons, told me:

> They need be allowed to ride bikes, climb trees, have scuffles with brothers and buddies, to be listened to and encouraged as they dream of their great adventures in the wild. When we protect them too much until it becomes stifling to their development as men, they can't learn the confidence they need in order to go out into a world that doesn't help anyone, to make a living and establish their own family.

What about in the grade-school years when our son comes in with blood pouring down his face from a small gash on his forehead because his attempt to jump from roof to tree didn't pan out, or from some other boyhood antic? They need us to not panic, to stay calm. (Later, after he's gone back outside, you can go to your bedroom and cry if you need to; we hate to see our kids hurt.)

They do need Mom to make sure the hurt doesn't need stitches, to wash and bandage it, to perhaps at some point ask them what they learned, and comfort them if they need it. But they don't need our overreaction or lectures. If we do lecture or say, "I told you so," they learn that we don't trust them or don't believe they have what it takes. In adulthood, men will need us to believe that they can "make it," because they long to feel competent. If not, they experience a terrible feeling of distress. Having what it takes to make it in life is the central need of adult males.[3]

Being Intentional About Developing Confidence

From the time her three sons were very young, Jennifer had in mind that she was raising men, not boys. *These little fellas are going to be grown someday,* she thought as she held each of her baby boys. *I want to raise men who are confident, so when they make a decision, they don't agonize and second-guess themselves.*

She had seen firsthand in her husband Wayne's life how a man struggles with making decisions when his determined, strong-willed mother dominates and criticizes him. In anything Wayne did or decided during his childhood, adolescence, and early adulthood, his mother had a better way: "This is how I would have done it" or "You made the wrong choice; I'm disappointed," she told her son over and over. So ingrained that he was going to make the wrong decision, throughout his life he agonized at every choice and bend in the road, fearful he'd make a mistake.

Seeing the results of this kind of mothering, Jennifer parented a different way: toward raising confident decision makers. *How can I teach my boys to trust their decisions?* she wondered early in Brantley, Kennedy, and Stinson's lives.

First, Jennifer looked for every opportunity to turn over decision making to her sons in an age-appropriate way. When they were toddlers, she told them, "Here are three outfits. Choose which one you want to wear." When they were old enough for sports, she let them decide what they would play. Wherever a range of options would work, she let her boys choose:

- To shower in the morning or at night
- To do homework after school or after dinner
- To wear mismatched shirts and pants or not, or even shirts inside out
- To wear a watch on the right wrist or the left
- To have scrambled eggs or fried

Second, she affirmed their decisions and backed them up even if she would have done things differently or it meant sacrificing her own convenience.

Many times, especially if one of the boys showed up in an unconventional outfit, she let others' opinions go because her larger purpose was to help her boys grow into confident, independent men. Along the way, she found there was a big range of things she could allow her sons to take over, and whenever possible gave them the freedom to do so and find their own way.

That doesn't mean Jennifer and her husband didn't provide guidance or discussion, discipline, and rules. They did. But when Jennifer was widowed at age fifty-two, and two of her sons were still in high school and one in college, she saw that the foundation of relationship and trust she'd built throughout their lives made a huge difference in their growing up into men who were ready to face the world even though their dad had died.

When a mistake was made, rather than lecture or say, "I told you so," her response was, "What could you learn from this?"

A barrage of nagging and lectures is not what sticks with guys of any age, especially from adolescence on. Genuine *conversations* are more impacting, so she discussed issues and decisions with her sons and encouraged them to think for themselves, to evaluate options, or make a pros and cons list if necessary to clarify a choice. *Should I play football this season or focus on a different sport even though both of my brothers are starters on the team? Should I keep dating this girl or break up? What college should I apply to?*

Like this mom, our basic message to our sons needs to ultimately be *I think you'll make a good decision.* There are other comments that develop confidence like "You decide," "You make the choice," "I'm comfortable with what you decide," and "You pick." Then back them up with remarks like "You did a good job picking that out," "You did some creative thinking to come up with that solution," or "I like that shirt on you."

As author Chick Moorman in his book *Parent Talk* says,

> When you qualify "You decide" by adding a condition, you give children criteria and require thinking. The condition gives them something concrete on which to base their decision. You help them develop their choice-making ability and thinking skills simultaneously.

For example, when your child asks, "Can I go outside to play?" you could respond, "If you'll remember to come in when it starts raining. You decide."[4]

41

There are some pitfalls to avoid if you want to raise confident sons. When your boy isn't a child anymore and gets into his adolescent years, offering help or advice *when he asks for it* is more effective than anticipating his problems and trying to solve them. In addition, it's best to avoid undercutting your son's actions by regularly saying things like "I don't think that's a good idea," "Don't do that," "Wait, you're not doing this right," "That's so difficult; let me do it for you," or "I'll talk with your teacher and get her to change your grade." This kind of language conveys to your son that he is always going to need you and he isn't capable of making it on his own.

"I often see that very involved moms get tripped up when their sons get into the teen years," psychologist Ken Wilgus told me. Further,

> They keep doing what they've been doing with their boys during the childhood years. When moms say or act like "I'm helping you or doing this for you because I don't think you can take care of yourself," it sends a signal of no confidence. The most common mistake I see is when mothers apply childhood techniques to adolescence; that offends teenage boys' sense of confidence and humiliates them.

"You'll Figure It Out"

One of the most confidence-building things you can say to a son—especially an adolescent or young adult—is "I know you'll figure it out." These simple but powerful words mean that Mom doesn't have to give him all the answers. She has all the confidence in the world in him. Eventually, as he gets practice in problem solving and figuring things out, he will become more resourceful and assured, realizing he doesn't have to run to Mom or Dad because *he is capable.*

This kind of attitude doesn't suddenly develop when our boys get the keys to the car or leave for college. It needs to start when they are much younger. As Leslie Vernick, counselor, mother, and author of *The Emotionally Destructive Relationship*, told me,

> Raising a confident, courageous boy involves letting them do things by themselves and make mistakes: Having your son make his bed without you remaking it. Pulling on his jeans alone as soon as he's able, even struggling to figure that out after you've shown him. Because ultimately if you're a good parent, you work yourself out of a job to the point that *your son doesn't need you*. That's healthy, effective parenting.[5]

We humans learn many things through failure. In fact, in a new study, students who were told a task was going to be difficult and that failure was common did much better than a group of students who weren't told the "failure is okay" message. The reason is that kids who think of failure as a step toward success feel freer to problem solve.[6] But if mothers have issues with failure, they won't let their boys grow and learn much. They can't walk unless they fall. They won't feed themselves unless we allow them to get oatmeal all over their faces and be okay with it.

Vernick adds,

> If we are so prideful, controlling, or shamed by their behavior, boys get the message that we don't have confidence in them. Then they don't have room to develop competency. Since the core identity for a man is to feel competent, one of the best gifts we can give our sons is to foster it.

Although we want things to go well for our kids and for them to be happy, the reality is that an easy, pampered life isn't always the best for our sons. In fact, the more they have opportunities "to struggle and learn to struggle well, the better off they will be later in life,"[7] according to therapists Stephen James and David Thomas. In order to develop character and learn to handle the rough spots, boys need to face some adversities.

When they are overprivileged and everything is given to them, we are doing them a disservice because guys don't develop the vital sense of "I can do this." Resiliency develops as boys wrestle through and solve problems. In the process, as they experience successes, failures, and consequences instead of being rescued or having everything fixed by their mothers, they will grow more confident in their own abilities and decision making.

It's also a great boost to your son's confidence to let him be helpful to you. Ask for *his assistance* instead of always being the one who helps—not just taking out the garbage, but important things: "Would you help me with my computer?" (or smartphone or installing a new app, Blu-Ray DVD player, etc.) or "You're better at this than I am." "Do you think this looks okay (after you've rearranged the living room)?" "Would you make this call to the cable company tech support and help me reset the DVR?"

At a restaurant, have your son tell the waiter what he'd like (instead of your ordering for him after he tells you what he wants). Give him practice on ordering for you or the whole group. By the time he is eight, he can also phone in the family's pizza delivery order or Chinese takeout. Jot down the details or provide a short script if he's hesitant or shy on the phone. Helping the family or taking care of his mother gives a son practice in learning how to care for the needs of a wife someday, plus it builds his confidence.

Another great way to encourage a young man's competence is to trust him now and then with a responsibility that surprises him. One family left their fifteen-year-old son on the farm to attend a local auction and bid on a tractor while they visited some friends thirty miles away. From being trusted to do this, the teenager had a boost in confidence and accomplished something his parents were proud of: He obtained an excellent tractor for a very good price.

Thinking Outside the Box: Pablo the Paint Horse

Aaron was born with a love for horses. Playing with plastic horses was fun for a few years, but since his family lived on a farm, he thought it was a great idea to have his own real horse. The summer after third grade, his grandpa bought him a horse named Lady and she became Aaron's best friend. He rode Lady, fed her, cared for her, and when he was thirteen decided to have her bred. When the foal was born, Aaron trained it by himself and became quite a horse whisperer.

This young teen decided to start his own business breaking and training horses. With his parents' permission, he put an ad in the rural papers. As it turned out, lots of people brought him horses to train. The budding entrepreneur gave the horses names and tamed them all, working long hours every day . . . until he met Pablo Picasso, a strange and stubborn paint horse. Aaron could get a saddle on Pablo but couldn't get him to do anything. Day after day, hour after hour, Aaron worked with the incorrigible horse, but he kept backing up into the gate, into the shed, into the garage. Instead of moving forward, he moved backward. He refused to be trained.

After many days, Aaron was at the end of his rope. *I just can't do this.* He went outside where his mom was and they sat on the trampoline. "I'm terrible at this. I'm going to quit," Aaron told her.

Kendra felt it was important not to sugarcoat the situation by saying, "It's fine. This will all work out okay," because it was clearly not working out. Her son was terribly frustrated and about to give up his whole business. She wanted to encourage him to keep going and not quit but at the same time help him deal with reality.

"I'm going to take all the horses back to their owners. I'm a failure and I can't do this," Aaron told her.

His mom listened and listened until he was finished talking. Then she shared the only story she could think of: how Thomas Edison, after over one thousand failed attempts, discovered the electric light bulb and many other inventions. She encouraged Aaron to ask God for help and added, "I think you can do this."

And then, although the only thing she knew about horses was that they had four legs and a tail, she asked, "I don't know if this will work, but have you thought about . . . ?" and they began to brainstorm with some out-of-the-box ideas. She knew she couldn't solve the problem, but she also believed Aaron had a special ability to work with animals and had it in him to figure this problem out.

She primed the pump and had confidence in him. Aaron persevered, tried different approaches, and within twenty-four hours came up with a solution that got the crazy horse to move forward and cooperate. He called the owner and told him how many days until Pablo would be ready, and sure enough, had him trained as he'd promised and took the check to the bank.

"When the boy comes up with the solution, it's a confidence builder. He has much more motivation to try his plan than if Mom gives the answer and tells him what to do," Kendra told me.

Aaron worked hard and continued his horse-training business throughout high school and college summers, up until the second year of veterinarian school. Along the way, he learned to manage a business. He had so many clients he had to rent out a place to board the horses and employed his younger brother and a neighbor girl to help, and they all made money. Today he enjoys a career as a veterinary doctor.[8]

Where We're Headed

It helps if we can keep the goal in mind: to work ourselves out of a job in order to raise independent boys who think and act for themselves *and* grow into confident men who can stand on their own two feet. Yet sometimes, with the best intentions, we circumvent this process.

When we make things too easy for our boys, they don't have a chance to learn the resiliency (meaning, how quickly people tend to recover from setbacks like losing a game, failing a test, or losing a job), endurance, and strength a man will need to cope with life's challenges. When we smooth over most of the rough spots, they don't get prepared for life in the real world.

Now, maybe you're thinking we mothers can't win for losing! But there's something we can learn from the stories in this chapter: We can kill our son's confidence by making things too easy for him, by hovering, overprotecting, and over-functioning. Because if we over-function, our sons will tend not to put forth the effort to help themselves. In fact, they'll under-function, which leads to what's called "learned helplessness"—being unable to do a task or thinking they can't, and thus they don't try. Keep the big picture and goal in mind and raise your son to have room to individuate (become a separate, distinct individual), to become a competent, courageous, independent young man and someday leave you.

Questions to Ponder, Journal, or Discuss

1. What experiences did you have in childhood or adolescence that fostered confidence?

2. What did your parents do to build up or weaken your confidence in making decisions?

3. When was a time you over-functioned or helped your son too much when he could have done something for himself?

4. When did you trust and empower him? What was the outcome?

5. *Grit* is a combination of perseverance, determination, and resilience. How can you help your son develop grit? Brainstorm with a few other moms.

6. What is a new idea or concept you gained in this chapter that you could apply to building your son's confidence?

7. Discuss these thoughts with a friend:

    • Frequently stepping in to protect your son from stress may hurt him in the long run. Why?

    • Overparenting leads to unmotivated, easily depressed boys who don't develop the ability to set a goal and put an action plan together to achieve it. What principles in this chapter can help you avoid overparenting?

4

A Mom Who Overcomes
Her Fears

Fear is a thief. It erodes our faith, plunders our hope,
steals our freedom, and takes away our joy of living
the abundant life in Christ.[1]

—Neil T. Anderson, *Freedom From Fear*

You may agree with the ideas in the last chapter, but more than
mental assent is needed. If your heart is filled with fear, it inter-
feres with your goal of building the one thing sons need: confidence and competency. So in this chapter, let's talk about our
hearts and the greatest barrier to freedom, faith, and joy: fear.

As mothers, we loved and fed our wonderful baby boys,
rocked them when they were fussy, carried and strolled them
until they could walk. We held them when they were sick. We
worried when they had problems at school, lacked friends, or
made bad choices. We wanted so badly to protect our boys from
bullies and dangers of every kind.

Yet this same protective, mother-bear kind of love that seems to come with the job description brings powerful emotions like fear and worry. Commonsense caution is a good thing, but when we are persistently anxious, our caring can turn to clinging. We lose sleep and become preoccupied with *what might happen* if we aren't there to manage things. Yet how can we not be anxious when:

The boy who used to be close to you and chatted about his day on the way home now seems withdrawn and depressed. He retreats to his messy bedroom and you have to talk to him through the closed door.

Your son's report card arrived, and he's failing all his classes.

Your middle-schooler is in the emergency room with a raging strep infection and high fever.

Your bright, curious son is seeking for a philosophy to embrace, but seems to be looking in all the wrong places.

Each of these situations causes a natural sense of worry. And even if you haven't experienced anything similar, the reality is we live in an age of anxiety where all it takes to push a mom's panic button is to read the latest headlines or listen to the nightly news: reports of missing children, outbreaks of meningitis, violence in schools. With 24/7 cable and online news, we hear everything that's going on in the entire world—the bus accident in Russia that killed dozens of children, the terrible news of abductions and murder. Our minds begin to be filled with thoughts like *How can I avoid that? How can I protect my son?*

Mothers worry about the health of their kids and the crazy world they're growing up in. Moms of adolescents are often afraid their kids may get entrenched with the wrong crowd, drugs, or alcohol. There are economic fears, uncertainty about our jobs, and fears about our own health, especially if we have a son with special needs: *Who will be there to take care of him if something happens to me?*

First-time moms tend to be especially anxious. The top six things new mothers fear are (1) their baby dying from SIDS, (2) being abducted, (3) having a high fever, (4) leaving him with someone, (5) under- or overfeeding, and (6) their child not meeting developmental milestones (holding his head up, walking, talking).[2] I heard a mom share at a mothers' group that when she had her first baby, the world shifted. Everything held the possibility as a source of danger.

What's a mother to do with all these concerns? I don't approach this subject from a trouble-free ivory tower of certainty. I know what it's like for my heart to experience terror: I began hemorrhaging in the sixth month of a pregnancy; we rushed our four-year-old son to the hospital because he couldn't breathe; for many months our son Chris was being targeted by snipers and rocket-propelled mortars during his tour of duty in Iraq.

I grew up primed for anxiety, with a devoted mother who was very protective and afraid, so I had a strong, almost inborn tendency to worry and be fearful. We also had experienced several tragic deaths in our family, including the death of my father when I was eleven and a dear friend when I was thirteen. A significant part of my journey has been about dealing with losses and facing my fears, and with God's grace overcoming them so I could live life as an adventure and allow my sons and daughter to do the same.

The Damage of Fear

Lawrence O. Richards wrote, "Both anxiety and worry spring from natural and legitimate concerns that are part of life in this world." But these legitimate concerns become destructive "when they do one or more of the following: (1) become dominating concerns in our life and lead to fear, (2) destroy our perspective on life and cause us to forget that God exists and cares, or (3) move us to drift into an attitude of constant worry and concern over a future we cannot control."[3]

In addition, when fear and anxiety are a mother's dominant emotions, it takes her out of the present. She tends to hover, overprotect, or over-control, which not only sabotages a healthy mom-son relationship, but can hinder her boy's growth and individuation process. By overcoming our fears, we help our sons overcome their fears and live in more freedom.

Control and fear are closely connected. The more fearful a woman is, the more controlling she acts and the more she dominates her children. When a mother fears her son won't be successful and pushes him constantly, it can lead to the opposite: underachievement. When a son is controlled by a dominant, fearful mother, it can lead him to depression, low self-worth, low self-confidence, dependency—and even a strong tendency to resent her and struggle with anxiety throughout his own life.

That's what happened to Matt, who had an emergency appendectomy when he was three years old. The surgery scared his anxious mother so much that the incident infected his whole life. She held on to every detail and rehearsed the dangers of surgery over and over with her son, feeding his fears before and after the operation. Yet even in his thirties and forties, although Matt couldn't actually remember the appendectomy, he and his mother talked about it as if it had just occurred.

As a result, Matt was desperately afraid of illness and overly preoccupied with his own health. He was a bright, kind, loving man, but always afraid of taking any risks, fearful of the future and what might happen to family members. He worried about his children getting sick or having to have surgery like he did. In adulthood, he worked hard to try to overcome these emotions, but because he was preprogrammed with a burdensome load of fear and anxiety, he continued to struggle throughout his life.

Draining Our Energy

But our children aren't the only ones whom fear affects. When we are controlled by fear and anxiety, we experience damage as well. Well-being is compromised, starting with our strength and energy.

One of the things we need most as mothers to care for our children and teenagers over the long haul—especially boys—is energy. Each of us has a certain supply of calendar energy, which means the emotional and physical resources we possess in a twenty-four-hour period. We need all the total calendar energy of each day to deal with our children, job, life, and all its demands. If we use these finite resources being fearful, we can run out of gas, become stressed, and burn out. Worst of all, we will lack the inner resources to be the mother we would like to be. I don't know about you, but I don't want to waste any of that much-needed energy!

Another resource we need as a parent is the ability to think clearly and make good decisions, both at work and at home. Fear causes confusion and faulty thinking. Our brains contain more than two billion megabytes of capacity to handle the challenges and problems of daily life. But when we're preoccupied with fear, thoughts become tangled. Inner strength and mental clarity are sapped. Logical and creative thoughts can actually be blocked. Chronically anxious people complain they can't concentrate and are easily distracted from finishing daily tasks.

If that's not enough, fear also steals our joy. If you're a visual person with a good imagination, your concerns and anxieties turn into mental videos that play in your mind's eye. Or you may replay your mental tape recorder over and over with negative messages and what ifs. In either case, it's difficult to be happy and fearful at the same time; while you may speak of being joyful in God, your children will not see that evidenced in your life. If your joy is drained away by fear about what might happen tomorrow, it empties you of the strength you need *today*.

Not Passing Along Our Fears

"One of the best things you can do to cultivate your son's maleness is to deal with your own fears in an appropriate way," says therapist Ruthie Hast. "One thing I regret is protecting my sons too much. A lot of overprotection came from my fears." When she drove her boys to the city, passing over a bridge, she feared she'd careen into the creek below and only be able to get one of them out. She felt sheer terror that someone would steal her beautiful little blond boys. "So I held their hands and kept them right next to me at the grocery store when I could have let them run two feet ahead of me," she added.

Ruthie began counseling with a therapist when her boys were ten and twelve for issues about her father's illness and death. This wise counselor advised Ruthie concerning her fears in various areas of her life and how this was a byproduct of her being overprotected throughout childhood. When one of the boys was seeing a counselor in his early teen years, his therapist helped address her fears as well.

When she was in graduate school and studying the needs of children in different developmental stages, Ruthie didn't have time to obsess about her sons. She talked to God who gave her the wisdom she needed in each instance and she did a lot of counting to ten and sending up arrow prayers—short prayers sent heavenward during the course of the day. The point here is that if we are frequently gripped by fear about our children, getting help may be the kindest thing we can do for our sons and ourselves. Consider therapy with a trusted counselor to deal with your own issues so you won't pass them on to your kids. Today Ruthie is an excellent counselor and life coach who is helping many families, children, and women in our community. She shared some advice to mothers who struggle with fears:

- Learn all you can about the needs of boys at each developmental phase. Be open to the fact that you don't know everything, and remain curious and teachable.
- Consider getting into a parenting group.
- Talk to older, wiser, experienced mothers you trust and admire for their parenting abilities.
- Relax! Chances are, if you're praying for your son and practicing wisdom, you aren't going to break or ruin him.
- Listen to your sons and don't take personally what they tell you. You might actually learn something from them.
- Remember your own upbringing and use what was helpful to you in maturing, but discard the rest.

I had an interesting interview with Ruthie's son Daniel, a bright thirty-two-year-old who loves his mother dearly and is her greatest fan:

Mom did try to shelter us, but she didn't totally succeed because my brother and I were too intrepid. But her fears did limit us, and there were things we didn't get to do that our buddies did because Mom sheltered us for her sake, not our sake. When I was a kid, I was aware she had some fears. And when a belief or fear or superstition comes from your parents, you unfortunately have no choice but to embrace it.

Daniel talked about liking to stay up and sleep as late as he could on the weekends. He'd always been a night owl and still is today. Starting in middle school, his mom told him, "You can't stay up all night; it will make you sick." So he tested the waters. Sometimes he stayed up twenty-four hours in a row and found out he'd be okay, just tired. "She had practically guaranteed me that if I stayed up too late I'd get sick," Daniel told me. "What I discovered was yes, I got tired, but not sick. Since I had grown up believing this and discovered it wasn't true, it was upsetting. It made me doubt other things she said."

When I asked him what his mom could have done differently, he said, "Rather than expressing her view as truth, she could have said, 'This is my feeling, my experience. This is why I don't stay up all night and don't want you to. I'm afraid I'll get sick and you will as well.'"

Daniel and other young men I interviewed said they found it frustrating and negative when their moms passed on fears to them. They felt there was enough for kids and teenagers to be stressed out and afraid of today. "So the last thing a mother needs to do is project her fears on her children," Daniel said. "They'll have their own things to be afraid of and on top of those, their mom's fears, so the stress load doubles." Daniel reflected further,

> It helps when there is a dad to balance out a cautious mother and encourage his son to be strong, be assertive, be bold. When she's being overly protective and wants to say, "Don't climb that tree or those rocks, you'll break your arm," the dad can say, "Let the boy go and break his arm. He'll only do it once." That's important. Boys need to test the waters and see what they are capable of. A controlling, protective mom doesn't allow him to do that.

Dealing With Your Fears

But what if you don't have a father present in the home to balance out your caution? It helps to seek other male input from your dad, grandfather, or uncle if they're really invested in your lives. Share what you're worried about and ask them to point out if you're reacting out of fear and holding your son back.

If you struggle with worry, phobia, fear, or anxiety, don't feel alone. Millions of people struggle with anxiety, and it affects twice as many women as men. It's the number-one emotional and mental health problem today.[4]

Again, I don't have all the knowledge on handling fear, but I will share my story of being a very anxious young mother who was afraid of many things, especially losing one of our children.

When our oldest was four years old, he began having severe asthma attacks. For two years, we were in and out of doctors' offices trying to figure out what Justin was allergic to and how to treat it. I was always looking for ways to keep him healthy and out of the hospital.

No matter what we tried, the attacks continued and I felt powerless. Most of the episodes landed him in the ER, followed by five or more days in the hospital until he could breathe normally and go home. It got to the point where we couldn't go out of town because even a change of climate or barometric pressure triggered an attack and another trip to the ER.

When Justin was six, yet another attack landed him in the hospital. This time the doctor said they had done all they could, but our son's body was filling up with carbon dioxide. If something in his body didn't rally . . . they had no alternative treatment. I was terrified. And at the advice of my husband, who said I was making Justin nervous, I went down to the hospital chapel and had a long talk with God, admitting I had put my hope in the doctor and the medicine and Holmes and me to save our son—that I had clung to my children, trying to keep them well and safe on my own. I asked God again to please heal Justin. I pleaded and cried and felt very alone, hearing only the sound of a rainstorm outside.

But what I heard in my spirit in those quiet moments was life-changing: *"Hope in me. Trust his life to me totally, now and always."* It was one of the hardest things I ever did, but as a thunderbolt crashed, I was reminded that the Creator of the whole universe—and our firstborn—was in complete command of the storm and could be trusted with Justin. In not releasing him to God's care, I realized I would be thwarting the very power that could help him.

I did exactly that: I entrusted and released our child to God, regardless of the outcome. A huge weight lifted inside me and I was flooded by a feeling of peace. In some inexplicable way I knew I could trust God with our son. An hour and a half later, when I walked into Justin's room, he was sitting up in bed, rosy cheeked and smiling, coloring a picture and breathing better than he had in days. Although he continued to have asthma, he was a varsity tennis player in high school and has run many marathons in his adult life.

To manage your fear and concern, it is essential to:

Pray for your children. In this situation and countless others, I learned that putting my energies into prayer and placing our three children in God's strong hands is the very best thing I can do for them. Time after time through the years, we have experienced the Lord's faithfulness in our lives.

That's why I can encourage you to do what goes against the grain of your mother instinct: Release, let go, entrust your son and all your children to God, who loves them even more than you do. Please note that when I say, "Let go of your son," I don't mean to let go of your responsibilities. I mean, entrust his life to the God of the universe, the Creator and Sustainer of all things and the One who made him and has a purpose for him.

Then in any situation or difficulty, think about what is your part, God's part, and your son's part, and avoid the pitfall of trying to control the outcome of things. Daily give God your burdens, one by one, writing them down if necessary, instead of being overwhelmed by them.

In the next chapter, we will look at the great need sons have for praying moms. Prayer is one of our most important ministries in our children's lives, even throughout their adulthood. I'll share how you can live a praying life in the midst of all your duties, mothering, tasks, and responsibilities so that you can give your children the greatest gift any mother can provide—the gift of covering their lives in prayer.

Get into God's Word and let faith replace your fear. Hundreds of verses in the Bible admonish us not to fear, worry, or be anxious. The major way to build a faith that will overcome our fears is expressed well in Romans 10:17: "Faith comes from hearing the message, and the message is heard through the word about Christ."

Each week, pick a verse that specifically applies to your son or your concerns. God's Word will help you stand firm and have a courageous heart in the midst of difficult times. It will help strengthen you so you can experience calmness instead of hysterics, peace instead of panic. The faith to trust God when we're afraid comes through applying the Scriptures to our lives. As we believe the Bible and know the Lord in a deeper, personal way, these God-breathed truths will break us free from fear.

If we say we are people of faith, our sons and daughters want us to "walk the talk," or live out in real life what we believe. We can be women who trust God instead of obsessively worrying, mothers of faith instead of being harassed by fear.

Let me encourage you that regardless of your circumstances, God doesn't want you to live in fear. He has a plan for you to enjoy the gift of life and the gift of your children for the brief time they are under your roof—as you trust Him and entrust your precious ones to His care.

Questions to Ponder, Journal, or Discuss

1. What concern do you have for your son that pushes your panic or worry button?

2. What circumstances feel out of your control?

3. Ask yourself: Am I protecting my son because there is a real danger or am I reacting out of fear or worry?

4. What is holding you back from putting your son in God's hands and letting go? What would you have to believe about Him to release your son to His care?

5. What blessings might you miss if you choose to hold on rather than entrust your son to the Lord?

5

A Mom Who Prays for Her Son

It is beyond our imaginations what prayer can effect
in the earth. When God's name and His renown are
the desire of our heart, our prayers for our children,
grandchildren, and descendants can be the catalyst
that will cause His fame to spread to all the corners
of the earth.[1]

—Jennifer Kennedy Dean, *Legacy of Prayer*

I got a letter recently from a mother who told me she wished
she had more time to pray for her children. But she was so busy
with a multitude of things, prayer time was absent from most
of her days. I understand what it's like to have a full plate. I
remember being a mom of three school-age children, teaching
high school part-time to make ends meet, and also helping at my
husband's interior design store. In addition, I was the driver for
sports practices and games, music lessons, and Alison's dance

classes. Laundry, housework, cooking, and writing magazine articles also took part of my day.

When could I possibly find time to pray?

I agree with what Fern Nichols, founder and president of Moms In Prayer International, said, "Every mother feels the need to pray for her child. And every child needs a praying mom."[2] Truly, in my travels in many states and countries around the world to speak at conferences—from Thailand to Singapore, Brazil to South Africa, and Switzerland to Zambia, I have yet to meet a mother who hasn't uttered a prayer for her children and desired the very best for them.

For me, it made all the difference when I caught a vision of the power, the invitation, and the longevity of prayer's impact. When I believed that prayer is one of the most important ways we can bless our children not only in the present but also throughout their lives, I had a more compelling desire to pray for them, to get up earlier, and to ask God to open up windows of time in my busy day to pray.

When I read Revelation 5:8 that speaks of the "golden bowls full of incense . . . which are the prayers of God's people" (AMP), I realized that our prayers are set before God and they don't go away when our physical bodies die or when our address changes to heaven. The truth is, our prayers will go on being answered in our children's lives, our grandchildren's, and other loved ones'. I love how minister and author E. M. Bounds put it: "The prayers live on before God, and God's heart is set on them, and prayers outlive the lives of those who uttered them, they outlive a generation, outlive an age, outlive the world."[3]

What a fortunate son it is who has a mother who covers his life in prayer! For truly, how can we meet all our son's needs? By leaning on the everlasting arms of Christ, by asking Him for wisdom, patience, love, discernment—and to give us a fresh vision of the power of praying for our children.

There may be a time of persevering and waiting until we see the fulfillment of our petitions. Yet the fruit of our prayers is worth the wait. Jennifer Kennedy Dean describes prayer as a "spiritual trust fund." In her book *Legacy of Prayer*, she explains,

> Prayer has no limits—no time limits, no geographical limits. Just as surely as we can provide for our children's present and daily needs through prayer, we can also reach into their futures, laying a foundation of blessings for our children, our grandchildren, and all of our descendants.
>
> Prayer is so effective that when our children are away from us, we can continue to parent them through our prayers. Our prayers are more powerful even than our presence.[4]

As these truths sunk in, I knew that praying for our sons and daughter was perhaps the best investment I could make in their lives apart from loving them.

Drawn to Prayer

I was also drawn to prayer in part because circumstances like our son's ER visits had made me aware early on that I was not in control. Thus when difficult times came, my concerns propelled me to turn to God. Over the years, I discovered and practiced different ways to pray for the kids: to take prayer walks, to pray with other women, to pray the Scriptures, and to persevere— Pray Until Something Happens (PUSH) and not give up.

I also had the blessing of learning from older women that no matter how much I loved my sons and daughter, took them to church, read the Bible and had nightly devotions with them, *only God* had the power and ability to shape their hearts into deciding to follow Christ. Yet that power could be released through a mother's prayers. Knowing this motivated me even more to make prayer an utmost priority.

In addition, one of the greatest truths I learned by experience was that there is a special power when mothers come together to pray in agreement (see Matthew 18:19–20). I started leading a Moms In Prayer group once a week for our kids and their school many years ago and continued for twelve years. What a joy it was to gather weekly with other mothers to pray for our children; it was the best-spent hour of my week. And when I didn't see answers to my own prayers, I was encouraged about how God was working in the other women's children through our corporate, weekly prayers for them.

Yes, like you, I had a hectic life. But as I grew in a relationship with God through His Word, I sensed Him saying to me as He did to Martha when she was very busy doing many things: "[Cheri, Cheri,] you're fussing far too much and getting yourself worked up over nothing. One thing only is essential" (Luke 10:41–42 THE MESSAGE)—and that one necessary thing is spending time with Christ through a prayerful life.

I found that the grace I experienced in the past wouldn't do for this new day I was facing with all its challenges. We need God's sustaining grace every day of mothering our children, and it is there to draw on. Oswald Chambers said, "Prayer is the exercise of drawing on the grace of God. Don't say, I will endure this until I can get away and pray. Pray now. Draw on the grace of God in the moment of need."[5]

The Power of Prayer

I love the way our pastor Matt Jones described prayer this week in his sermon. He said that in prayer, Jesus holds your hand and the Father's hand at the same time. As Holmes and I have prayed for Justin, Chris, and Alison and for our grandchildren, we've seen God work in countless ways. For example, when Chris was at the University of Oklahoma as a premed student, I didn't know what to pray for him. Our quiet, reserved son was never brimming with personal information, so I didn't know what was going on in his life. I was baffled and needed new direction. I asked God one morning, "Please give me a verse from the Bible that directs my prayers and reflects your heart for Chris."

A few nights later I had a dream so vivid I've never forgotten it, though I rarely remember dreams. In it, Chris was standing beside me, all six-foot-three of him, looking down at the Bible he was holding. He pointed to a verse in Acts that read, "In Him we live and move and have our being" (17:28). In my dream, Chris said, "Mom, that's me. That's who I am."

I wrote the verse down when I woke up in the morning and knew it was the answer to my prayer—not only to specifically pray this for Chris but also to ask God to reveal that this describes who he is. I've prayed it many, many times since then . . . through college and medical school, while Chris was serving as a navy doctor during the war in Iraq, during his residency, and now as a practicing dermatologist with a wonderful wife and two daughters.

Another outcome of a significant long-range prayer for our oldest son, Justin, occurred at the end of his sophomore year of college. I'd been praying for six years for Justin's heart to turn back to following God without seeing any movement in that direction. Day by day, week by week, I kept praying for him. After finals in May, he moved back home but had no prospects for a summer job.

Following dinner that night, Justin asked me to drive him across town so he could have his overheated car towed. On the way, he talked about his frustrations and how the relationship with his girlfriend had gone sour. Then he turned and said, "Mom, I've been feeling empty and lonely, living so far from God and trying to do everything on my own. I know that God hasn't moved. I have. But I want more than anything to have an intimate relationship with Christ."

My heart leaped so with joy I could have jumped out of the car. Our son's life took a 180-degree turn toward Christ. Opportunities opened up for him; he grew in his faith over the months, and he's never looked back.

The more I saw God work through prayer, the more committed I became. For I knew that a mother's prayers build the bridge that links heaven and earth and lay down the tracks for God's limitless power to come in our sons' lives. If we'll do our part, He will do His—and as the love of a mom's heart for her son and God's love for this child connect, something dynamic happens.

Casting Your Cares and Burdens on Him

One of the best parts of prayer is the invitation to give God our burdens. As a young mother, I had a lot of these! In my second pregnancy, I went through labor and delivery, but the baby boy died a few minutes after delivery because his lungs weren't developed enough to survive. I was often concerned about my older sister, who struggled with depression and alcoholism for many years. When I was thirty-four, my mother was diagnosed with a virulent form of cancer and died four months later, which was heartbreaking. Within a few years, my husband began struggling with serious depression.

Like any other mother, I also had the normal concerns about my kids—when they were sick with some nasty virus that blew through the school, when one of them was struggling with a subject, didn't make the team, broke his collarbone, or had no friends at a new school.

When I first discovered Psalm 55:22, "Give your burdens to the Lord, and he will take care of you" (NLT), and 1 Peter 5:7, "Cast all your anxiety on him because he cares for you," I took the words to heart. As I studied the Amplified version of the Bible, I found 1 Peter 5:7 really means, "Casting the whole of your care [all your anxieties, all your worries, all your concerns, once and for all] on Him, for He cares for you affectionately and cares about you watchfully." When I read those words, I thought it was one of God's greatest, most gracious invitations.

Here's the problem: We self-sufficient, capable women often don't accept this marvelous invitation and keep carrying our own burdens with an attitude of "I'll do it myself." The more we carry our burdens, stress and anxiety can build as we think, *I can and should do this all myself (or should have fixed the problem).* These thoughts bring depression and overwhelming anxiety.

When we cast our cares on God through prayer instead of lugging them around in our emotional backpacks, He doesn't turn us away or say, "I'm too busy running the universe; you handle this problem." Instead, He makes a great exchange: peace that guards our heart and mind from anxiety (Philippians 4:6–9); a promise to be our refuge and strength in troubled times (Psalm 46:1); and wisdom we need as mothers (James 1:5).

I've found that we can even begin to see pressures and burdens as not just something to harass and disturb us—but as a call to prayer. Lawrence O. Richards wrote, "Anxiety, rather than drawing us away from God, draws us to him and thus fulfills his purpose for it in our lives."[6]

Is there a person or situation you need to "cast" upon God? Does your son have a great need in his life? Is there a problem that seems to have no solution? Lay that burden before God. I often pray the prayer in F. B. Meyer's *The Secret of Guidance*, because it is a wonderful way to turn everything over to God:

> Lord, I entrust to You this, and this, and this. I cannot carry them; they are crushing me, but I definitely commit them all to You to manage, and adjust, and arrange. You have taken my sins. Take my sorrows, and in exchange give me Your peace, Your rest.[7]

Once we release the burden to Him, and we're no longer managing and controlling, then God can do marvelous things—even more than we could imagine or hope for (Ephesians 3:20–21). He can change hearts, beginning with our own, and work things out in His way and His timing.

A good example of this happened in a prayer group Fern Nichols was in, in which they prayed with a mom who was distraught over her relationship with her son. Fern said,

> He hated her so much he would wince at her touch. The wall between them was high and wide. We prayed week after week for the relationship to heal. We asked God to tear down the wall of bitterness, resentment, and anger. We prayed that the mom would see things she might be doing that kept her son on the other side of that wall.
>
> By the end of the school year, the son was hugging his mom before he left for school. Who changed? I'm sure the mom would say that God changed her and that enabled her son to change, but truthfully, God changed them both.[8]

Weaving Prayer Into Your Daily Life

If you are bored with prayer . . .
If you are short of time . . .
If you have run out of words . . .

Then this section is for you! No matter how many tasks are on our to-do list, prayer is meant to be our loving lifeline. Once we realize this, we will make time for what is most important and valuable.

As I experienced the freedom that comes from giving God our burdens, I found ways to weave prayer into the hours of the day. Here are some ways to expand your connection with the Lord and your prayer life:

Let the events of your day be springboards to connect and converse with God. When you're on a plane and hear a child wailing in the seat behind you, send up a prayer for that child and mother. When you pass a handicapped parking place at your son's school, pray for the students who are disabled or confined to a wheelchair. When you stop for a funeral procession, pray for comfort and peace for the grieving family. When your son has a situation that you can't change, lift that to God and ask that His tenderhearted mercies would quickly meet his needs. These prayers may only take a few moments, but they help you stay in contact with God and impact the world around you.

When you're "prayed out" and clueless about what is the right way to proceed, look to Scripture. There are hundreds of verses in the Bible that are ideal for praying for sons because they reflect God's will and His best for him. Ephesians 1:17–18 has been the basis of a frequent prayer for our sons and now grandchildren through the years:

> I pray that you would give my sons a spirit of wisdom and revelation in the knowledge of God and that the eyes of their hearts may be enlightened, so they will know what is the hope of your calling for them and the riches of your glory and the surpassing greatness of your power toward those who believe.

More verses to pray are Psalm 119:11, Colossians 1:9–12, Proverbs 3:5–6, Jeremiah 29:11, Isaiah 54:13, and one of my favorites to pray, Psalm 5:12: "Lord, surround [my son] with your favor as with a shield." Every boy and girl, man and woman, needs God's favor to shine on them at school, at their job, in sports, in everything they do. This is a great way to bless your son in whatever stage of life he is.

Each year as you let Scripture shape your prayers, ask God to show you what is on His heart for your son and a specific verse that expresses this. Then be willing to follow how the Spirit would direct you to pray. It may be in a different direction than you ever would have thought, but as you pray Scripture and watch God work, you'll be encouraged and never run out of things to pray.

Let visual things be prayer prompts. When you pick up those size two or twelve Nike Air shoes in the living room after almost tripping over them, let them be a reminder to pray that your son's feet will stay on the right path. When you drive by his school and see the yellow Slow—School Zone sign, let that serve as a reminder to pray for wisdom for the teachers. You have to slow down anyway, so weave prayer into those moments. Remember, short prayers uttered in small pockets of time can accumulate to make a significant impact. And the more you pray, the closer your walk with Christ and the more grace you'll experience.

Pray on the spot when your son has a need—after you've listened well. A wonderful way to show your care and to connect with God's love for your son, especially when he's shared something he's upset or worried about, is to listen . . . listen . . . listen, and when he is finished talking, gently ask, "Could I wrap a prayer around that need?" Then pray a short, conversational prayer specific to the need or problem he expressed. Avoid a prayer that delivers a small sermon to your son: "O Lord, help John to be more interested in youth group and reading his Bible." (He will run from prayer if you do this.) Instead, thank God for something specific about your son and then lift up the need or request.

Be aware of how you are wired spiritually and pray in ways that help you connect with God—and you won't get bored with prayer. Not every woman talks to God best in the same chair at the same time every day. When we get out of the box and consider how we are designed, it makes prayer more of a delight and less of a duty. If you are a nature lover and love the outdoors, sit on your porch and be inspired by the sound of the birds and the wind (instead of distracted by the ringing of a phone or a noisy dishwasher in the house).

If you're active and think best when you're moving, carry your major requests for your son on an index card and set out to walk and pray. Or post the card on the treadmill and pray as you exercise. Prayer walks have been some of my best times with God in certain seasons, and it renews my heart as well as energizes my body.

Journal your prayers for your son if that works for you and helps you pour out your heart and petitions, hopes and concerns. Writing prayers is a helpful way to stay focused. Also record the answers when they come.

Make time for God; it's one of the best investments you'll make for your own life and for your children. You'll be emotionally and spiritually healthier and experience more joy when you stay personally connected to your Creator. Just like you schedule an appointment with a girlfriend to meet at Starbucks, make time for communion with the Lord.

If Your Son Is Headed for Destruction

Maybe you've felt like the mother I met last fall who tearfully told me she'd run out of ways to pray for her son, and he was still running headlong in a negative, destructive path. If so, tucked in the small book of Hosea is a passage that can inspire powerful prayer, especially for those times we feel helpless to influence a difficult situation.

If you read the story of Hosea and his wife, Gomer, you'll see how she was constantly unfaithful and running after lovers. So Hosea pledged to block her path with thornbushes, so she couldn't find her way. She'd chase and look everywhere, but not be able to find them. Hosea's hope was that his wife would then return to her husband. While this book of the Bible is a word picture of Israel's unfaithfulness to God and His love for them, it is also a great prayer prompt.

When your son doesn't have the wisdom to see the destructive path he's on, and your heart is breaking, turn to Hosea 2:6–7 and pray: "God, I ask you to build a hedge of thorns around my son to separate him from any influence outside your will and from those who would lure him into evil. May they lose interest in him. Also place a hedge to keep him from contacting those who have a dark and negative influence. Cause him to lose interest in them." Although this is not a formula, prayed persistently, this prayer can form a double hedge through which the wrong influences of people or things cannot pass. Then we ask that in his frustration, our son will turn to God.

Whether you call on God early in the morning or late at night, He will be listening when you pray. The truth that God listens to my prayers wherever I am didn't sink in until my son Chris left to attend a university twenty hours from home. Oh, how I missed hearing his voice! Busy with classes, intramural basketball, and studying, Chris didn't call often and there were no cell phones then. But once in a while, the phone would ring and it would be Chris. I'd drop everything—the book project I was working on, dinner preparations, sleep—just to hear his voice. Then when Chris was in Iraq for nine months of service, I only got to talk to him three times. They were in high-security combat zones and communication was limited. Oh, what a joy it was when he called.

One day I realized God feels the same way about you and me, only hundreds of times more, because although we're mothers, we're also his children (John 1:12). Whether walking, driving across town, or sending a prayer heavenward from your computer, He delights in hearing from you—not just once a day, but whenever you call.

Questions to Ponder, Journal, or Discuss

1. What has been your experience with prayer? When was the last time you prayed for your son and what was the outcome?

2. What is an answer to prayer that was surprising and different from how you thought things would work out—yet better than you could have imagined?

3. Is there someone in your family or life who prayed for you and you have felt the power of the blessing they passed on to you?

4. What is your biggest barrier to the prayer life you'd like to have?

5. If you could ask God for one thing that you feel is your son's biggest need, what would it be?

6

A Mom Who Listens
and Communicates

> God's plan is for a boy to learn the tools of communication from his mother and watch his father model them in his marriage.[1]
>
> —John and Helen Burns

A little boy came home from kindergarten. His mother was bustling around the kitchen, preparing lunch for a few friends. Matt followed her around, pulling on her skirt, trying to tell her what happened on the playground.

"Mommy, I was on the monkey bars and Jake ran up and hit me and I fell off the bars and didn't know what to do so I—"

"I'm behind, honey, and I've got to get lunch fixed," she replied as she kept cutting up celery and turned around to whip the cream. Her son followed her, trying to share his story.

"Here's the picture I drew. Look!" Matt said.

"In a few minutes, honey, when I get finished. . . ."

The boy kept on talking, launching into another story. Then he asked, "Mommy, are you listening?"

"Sure, honey," she said as she turned off the mixer and started setting the table.

Finally, Matt stopped her. She stooped down and they looked at each other, eye to eye. As his mom repeated, "I was listening," the boy put his little hands around her cheeks and asked, "But, Mommy, would you listen with your face?"[2]

That's a genuine need of a boy of any age, five to twenty-five, six to sixteen and way beyond: *to be heard*. Men never outgrow this need—that when they have something to say, a question to ask, or a thought they want to share, their mothers (and later, their wives) will listen with their faces, their full attention, and with their hearts.

Over many years of raising boys and having grandsons, I've seen how important it is for moms to have a listening ear and truly care about what they are saying—even when it's a rambling toddler's story. Filling this need can be challenging! Not because we don't care what our boys have to say, but because as women, we get distracted or are multitasking. And we tend to talk more than we listen. Before long, we wonder why our kids won't talk to us.

A Mother's Role

One of the most important roles of a mother is to help her son learn to communicate and express himself. We can be a mentor and guide in this area, but it all starts with our learning to listen.

Here are some simple things to apply to be a better listener to our kids:

- When your child is talking, put away your smartphone, give eye contact, and pay attention to his words, facial expression, and body language.
- Start small. Instead of setting a goal of listening to your son for an hour each day, start spending five minutes a day giving him your undivided attention.
- Be available to listen at random times, day and night. And be willing to hear about sensitive subjects without major overreaction. When you freak out about what your son tells you, he tends to clam up and not share anything significant.
- Ask open-ended questions. Closed questions that require only a yes or no answer don't stimulate conversation. Open-ended questions don't have a right or wrong answer. For example, instead of "How was school today?" you could ask, "What was your favorite part of the day?" and "What was the downer today, or your least favorite part?"
- When it's a problem or conflict your son is describing, silently pray for wisdom and patience so you'll know a good way to respond when that moment comes.

The way you communicate with your son—both through talking and listening—is important to his development and emotional well-being. As educator and author Chick Moorman wrote, "There is an undeniable link between the words you speak and your child's behavior and attitudes. The way you talk affects their perceptions, interpretations, beliefs, values, and approach to life; it influences their actions as well as the consequences of those actions."[3]

Paying Attention

Just yesterday when I was sitting in a local restaurant, I saw a mother, a younger child, and two teenagers in a booth nearby.

While they waited for their food, the mom texted the whole time, and right after the hamburgers and fries were delivered, she answered a call and talked for a while before returning to texting. Through the twenty minutes they were sipping their sodas and having lunch, there was great opportunity for conversation. Yet very little face-to-face interaction or communication actually took place between the mother and her children.

Although kids today are used to distracted parents (and are distracted by technology themselves), and we could think this is the norm, what message is this behavior conveying to kids about their value and who is the priority?

Now don't get me wrong. I like my iPhone and MacBook and use them frequently. But the truth is, if we are not willing to put our electronic devices away and engage with our kids and really listen, it will be hard to raise a son who listens.

"Listening communicates you're valuable to me and worth my time, which is an important message to give a child or teenager," Leslie Vernick told me. "It means your son is important to you and what he's saying to you is more important than talking on the phone, texting, or being on the computer. It's not that you have to be at their beck and call, but that you need to make time to listen and talk together."

In those situations when your son wants to talk and you can't stop what you're doing, you could say something like "Hold on. I can't listen right this minute because I've got to do this. Could you wait a few minutes?" and then find a window within a reasonable time to get back with him. It's the overall pattern of being willing to listen and care about communicating that matters.

Screen time and media input/digital device time needs to be monitored, including your own. "Young people today are just as addicted to their smartphones as addicts are to a drug," says high school teacher Eddy Helker. "To engage someone mentally, you can't multitask and try to talk while texting; it just doesn't work."

If we're always plugged in, our sons may resist having a "no cell-phone zone" during dinner. We can model a balance of technology and screen times and times without technology by letting our kids see us reading, eating, working, volunteering to help others, making things, and being outside—all without digital devices. It helps to come up with your own healthy boundaries that fit your family and your individual children.

Talking About a Son's Interests

One of the keys to communicating with boys, especially preteens and teenagers, is to make the effort to talk about their interests and things that affect them (school, sports, friends).

With three girls and five boys, Cindy, a South Carolina mother, found boys related differently, especially in conversation. The key she discovered was to plug in to what mattered to her boys, which was unique to each of their interests. For example, Jeremiah's passion was cars and trucks.

While taking a trip to Atlanta, Jeremiah told his mom how important it was for her to recognize what kind of trucks were coming toward them. When he found out she had no idea, he began teaching her how to recognize what to look for in each truck's make and model.

"He quizzed me on every truck that came toward us or beside our car," said Cindy. "I realized it was important that I listen and focus on what he was saying and really look at the trucks, even if I don't give two hoots. In that moment, I needed to be a good listener and be engaged in what he cared about."

Especially between the ages of twelve and fifteen, when sons are no longer little boys but are entering into the stage of manhood, they want and need a mom who listens. "If we don't listen then, they won't talk to us down the road," Cindy said.

Thinking for Himself

We often spend more time talking to our sons—giving instructions, teaching, lecturing, telling them what to do and when to do it—than listening to them. But when we do listen and encourage our son's thought process, it has a positive impact. We might even see a tiny glimpse into his heart and mind.

A young acquaintance named Zack told me,

> One of the best things my mom did for me was to encourage me to think for myself. She allowed my mind to develop and let me pursue my own ways of thinking—my brothers too. This was a good thing—to let us think for ourselves, rather than having to parrot what our parents or others were saying. Many of my friends' parents tried to think for them and get their kids to think just like they did.

Zack's mother guided her sons in thinking objectively, but didn't insist that they had to agree with her. They discussed things and she'd ask, "What do you think about this?" Then they'd chase a rabbit down a rabbit trail and discuss all sides of an issue. Not only did Zack and his brother grow up to be thinking, decisive men, but they have continued in dialogue and conversation with their mom over the years.

My daughter-in-law Tiffany, who is a counselor and also the mother of our grandson Caleb, finds that by the time boys are twelve years old, they have heard just about every parenting axiom we could say. So if your son comes to you with something he wants to talk about, listen first. Avoid always being the one doing all the talking with an attitude of "Let me share/advise/

teach you." Likely the lecture will close the conversation, or his mind will be out of the room within a few seconds.

Boys need active listening from their moms, to hear not only their words but the whole message they are sending. Then you can summarize in a few words what you heard before jumping in to react or change the subject. This active listening communicates respect and interest and encourages him to know Mom is a safe place.

Next, focus on understanding the message rather than interrupting and giving answers, spouting rapid-fire advice, or telling him why he is wrong and needs to change. It's always worth the effort, because when we actively listen, we begin to understand how the other sees a situation.

The important thing is to keep communicating and listening so that a big Niagara–Falls–size gap doesn't develop between you and your son. Sometimes, as our boy grows out of childhood and passes through adolescence, he may not be into having deep conversations with his mother. He may get his advice from Dad, a mentor, or a coach, which is quite normal.

While you may miss giving your advice and opinions, don't panic. Give your son space. Know that love consists of more than words. There are things like silence, hugs, acceptance, and respect that can communicate the most. And have hope: There will be other times of communication down the road, and sometimes they happen when you least expect them.

Tips for Communicating With Boys and Teens

A son needs a mom who understands a boy's differences related to communication. When counselors engage a boy in conversation, they communicate differently than they do with a girl. Girls are generally more comfortable talking about their feelings, while boys are not—although there are always exceptions. Boys fear being shamed or looking weak, perhaps influenced by the cultural myth or family tradition that strong guys don't express their feelings. But if you give them a problem to be solved, they like to talk about that. Boys enjoy being consulted.[4]

Dan Kindlon and Michael Thompson write,

> Using a son as a consultant does not mean doing everything he wants. Absolutely not. But it does mean giving him a hearing. It helps if you have been doing it since he was young, because the practice you have shared together of talking, listening, and consulting will have helped your son know what is good judgment and what is not. If you listen to him seriously, he'll listen to himself seriously.[5]

Avoid shaming your son. If your son says or indicates that he does not want to talk with you at a certain time, "try to avoid saying or doing anything that might shame him for his refusal," says William Pollack. Shaming a boy leads to resentment and a hardening of his heart. "Saying things like 'Oh, you're just like your father,'" . . . is a shaming statement. "As much as you may feel rejected—or eager to help him—try to avoid punishing him for his decision to spend time alone."[6] Let your son know you're there for him if he does want to talk and that you love him.

Accept brief answers. As mothers of boys, we don't need to be surprised when we ask a question and get a very short answer. If we ask our son, "Why did you do that?" we may get no answer at all because he may not know in that exact moment the "why" of his behavior. If we can be accepting of their concise answers and avoid pushing them to share more, they may be more open to talking at some point. If we dig, and ask so many questions they can't even remember them, much less respond, they tend to avoid us.

For example, you can usually discern if your son has had a hard day. We get all concerned and want him to pour out his heart to us so we can have a long philosophical or encouraging discussion. But one male characteristic is that they don't necessarily want to talk about what happened on cue; if they're forced to, it may humiliate them or expose their weaknesses. If your son seems upset or disturbed, he may not even be in touch with why he's upset or precisely how he is feeling at that moment. He may need some time to think about what happened.

When sons do talk, they usually want to get to the point in a minimum of words. They want us to be concise. As my son asked me to do one day, "Please keep it simple, Mom." I tended to overtalk, to explain too much, to make sure they understood me. I can tell you from experience, they don't want us to keep hashing over the situation or our major points (*especially not* later in front of other people) or to over-dramatize.

Respect his privacy. A son needs a mother who is his trusted confidante. However, sometimes without realizing it, we break their trust. Mary's son shared an embarrassing situation that had happened in the locker room before basketball practice and how he felt about it. The next day after he'd slipped in the front door from school, he heard his mom on the phone in the kitchen going on and on, telling her friend all about what had occurred. He determined right then and there not to confide in her anymore. We may think it was a cute and positive thing we heard our son say, but they do not like us to talk to our friends about them and repeat their words. Guys are saying, "Please be confidential about what I tell you, Mom!"

Be calm and carry on. If you're emotionally upset and your voice is escalating by the minute, your son won't be able to hear what you're trying to say. He may stay in the room if he has to, but inside he'll withdraw and shut you out. You will find more about this subject and how to stay calm and loving in the midst of conflict, while helping your son deal with his emotions, in chapter 11.

Avoid the conversation buster of interrupting your son or finishing his sentences. Nothing shuts a boy's communication down faster than not being able to complete his own thoughts. Let's face it, most of us are guilty of this because we may think faster or *think we know* what our son is going to say. (This shuts down communication for grown men too.) While many boys today are great with technology, they may not be as fluent with talk. They need all the help they can get by being allowed to finish their own sentences even if it takes a few minutes extra to do so and by being encouraged to speak for themselves.

Avoid communication-control battles by clarifying whether the information being asked for is *required* or just *requested*. For example: For most years of adolescence the questions "Where are you going?" "When will you be back?" and "Who are you going with?" are not requested, they are required.

In this situation, mothers shouldn't be afraid to make it clear that unless this information is provided, the teenager will be given consequences (not allowed out, phone taken away, etc.). By the same token, when the information being sought is *not* required (e.g., "How was your day at school?") it is very important that moms start right out by clarifying, "You don't have to tell me anything you don't want to."

By defining which communication is required and which is not, control battles can be avoided. A teenager who hears that his mother knows she can't—and won't—make him tell her about his day is more likely to volunteer information. On the other hand, a mother doesn't gain anything by "being nice" and avoiding establishing clear consequences for required information being withheld.[7]

Allow questions and disagreement. When parents don't let their children disagree because they (Mom and Dad) are *always* right, it's a sign of over-control and tends to shut down conversation. Kids think, *Mom doesn't care about my opinion and won't let me express my views, so why try?* Then when something big comes up that he should be talking about with his parents, he thinks, *They weren't interested then, so why bother?*

If questions are discouraged, independent thinking is squelched. Then there is no chance for disagreement or discussion of different ideas, and the possibility for conversation decreases dramatically. As a result, boys lose their desire to talk with you. It is much better to ask, "What do you think of this issue?" "How should we approach this problem?" or "What are you thinking?" You don't have to do what they say or change your own mind, but your son will feel respected when his ideas are considered to have value.

Don't treat your teenage son like a child. A common reason teenagers stop communicating with their moms is that they are still talking to them as if they are children. They also get tired of hearing "I told you so," which makes them feel like a failure or having guilt heaped on them.

"Many moms can barely have a whole conversation with their adolescent sons without teaching, reminding, belittling, scolding, or cautioning," psychologist and counselor Ken Wilgus told me. Also,

> Mothers need to remember that he is a young adult and isn't
> sharing with the same desire to gain information from a parent

like a child does. She needs to recognize this change in his status and be cautious about when and how she offers advice.

Have you ever been tempted to rummage around in your son's room? "It's important to avoid the temptation to snoop," Wilgus advised. Further,

> The exception to this rule is when drug or alcohol use is strongly suspected (not intuition but real evidence). Moms too often try to fill in the gap of feeling out of touch from their adolescent sons and not knowing what's going on with them by reading texts, emails, and notes found in pockets or personal space. This usually leads to "white knuckle" information—that a mom finds out, but because she's not supposed to have been looking, she can't do anything about.

It's hard when we've had such good communication and relationships with our sons during their childhood, where they would sit on our bed and pour out their hearts—and then they go into the "cave" of adolescence.

As Ruthie Hast told me,

> During the teen years most boys are so not like girls. Many become secretive and apparently distant, but are testing their manhood. They're learning that they can discover relationships themselves. They are defining their "self" apart from their family of origin, which can seem like death to us relational moms. We have to keep reminding ourselves that they are not like us in this area and they need to be confident in their autonomy. They need us to not take it personally and to remember "It's not all about me!" Sons usually come back around to connection and more communication *after* they've become independent adults. So we need to be able to tolerate, for a time, what feels like rejection.

Good Conversations

"Some of the best conversations I've had with Caleb (twelve) have been when we're side by side: either playing tennis or shooting hoops in the driveway. Or at night when he's going to bed and I spend time sitting by him and he gets quiet and stuff just comes up to chat about . . . nothing planned and no agenda," my daughter-in-law Tiffany says.

She finds at this stage of preteen and adolescence, her kids' lives are so much more active, it's vital to be attuned to where they are and when moments open up, to be quiet and listen. "Both Caitlin and Caleb are so unique, constantly redefining themselves, changing, growing, and having new awareness, so we need to stay tuned in—and then be ready for unexpected moments to connect.

"When I plan a talk, let's say with a great conversation question to discuss while we're playing cards, it's usually over in thirty seconds. But there are times Caleb (or Caitlin) brings something up and it becomes a forty-five-minute conversation. It's about being available," Tiffany added.

As I share in the next chapter, often my best times of communication with our boys were when we were building with blocks when they were young or taking them by the hand and walking to the park together, throwing a baseball when they were a little older or hitting tennis balls when they were in junior high or high school, or playing Ping-Pong in the garage. The same thing is true with our grandsons. When I throw a football with them, play a game, or walk to the park, they often open up and share their thoughts.

I have seen in our sons and grandsons what family therapist Michael Gurian points out in *The Purpose of Boys*: "Talk and emotionality generally follows action and doing."[8]

Lively conversations can also come from creative or quirky questions, especially when your son is of elementary age.

These and similar questions are good to ask now and then (not all at one time) when you're in the car, on trips, or just hanging out:

- What would you like to be when you grow up? What would you NOT like to be?
- What's your favorite game, book, video, or movie?
- What would you do if you were in charge of the world?
- If you could go anywhere in the universe, where would it be?
- If you could drop one course/sport you're in right now, what would it be?
- What do you need from me at this time in your life?
- What are you fascinated with and want to learn about more than anything? (This is a question about one's center of learning excitement, and it's a key to motivation and conversation.)

When spoken words aren't working, use simple notes or whiteboards to communicate: random affirmations, reminders, quotes from great leaders. Write an annual birthday letter to your son, expressing your appreciation and love for him, your hopes and dreams, and bless him with words on his special day. Let your words bring life and keep sharing love and acceptance, and you'll be helping your son become a man who is caring, kind, and is developing skill in communication.

For many children, the world can seem like a very scary place and the future quite uncertain. That's where mothers and fathers come in, to help moderate the normal, predictable fears, disappointments, and heartaches of childhood and adolescence. Shared time, talk, and having someone to listen to you are often the very best medicine for the struggles involved in growing up.

Questions to Ponder, Journal, or Discuss

1. Next time your son is upset but won't talk about it, what is something you learned in this chapter that you could do differently?

2. What are some things parents do that shut boys down from talking or trying to communicate?

3. Were you allowed to freely express your opinions, and your parents "agreed to disagree" if they weren't on the same page, when you were growing up?

4. What works best as a place or situation where you and your son naturally talk?

5. Are you (and your son) a talker and more extroverted, or quieter and more introverted? What difference does this make in your communication?

6. What are your boundaries for your children with regard to technology?

7

A Mom Who Stays Connected

> There never has been, nor will there ever be, anything quite so special as the love between a mother and a son.
>
> —Unknown

I recently read a great idea from a dad who was a very busy, successful executive with platinum status on several airlines from his frequent business travel. When his oldest son turned nine, he realized that not only was his own life in fast-forward, but the time until his boy left home for college was getting shorter. He decided that he needed a way to better consider the passing of time, so he bought two glass jars. In one he put 468 colored marbles, one marble for each week until his son turned eighteen.

Every week he moved one marble from the full jar to the other jar. And today, 250 marbles later, his son is fourteen and only four years away from his departure.

This weekly, concrete countdown helped this parent stay focused on what was really important, on the goals he had and what he wanted to teach his son to prepare him for life.[1]

Not a bad idea for moms! Many are as busy or busier than this father. I remember feeling time pressures when our kids were at home. One day I was racing into the pharmacy, with my three-year-old son in hand and our eight-month-old son in my arms, to pick up a prescription, Tylenol, and a few groceries. We'd spent the morning at the doctor's office because one of them had a virus, and my to-do list was longer than my arm, with family coming in to town. There was laundry to do, dinner to cook, and housework along with the general care of the boys.

I gathered up our stuff and was waiting impatiently in the checkout line to pay when an older woman came up behind me. "Slow down and enjoy your boys while they are so young," she gently said to me (maybe she could sense my hurry-up attitude?). "The time will go so fast. My two sons are now grown and live on different coasts. How I miss them and wish I could spend just a day with them," she told me. Maybe you've received similar advice from an older mom. I have certainly shared it on occasion.

Days seemed to move slowly when the boys were little, but I knew the woman was right—that they would be grown before I knew it! Taking her words to heart, when I got home that day and on many other days, I put the work temporarily aside, sat down, and made Lego forts and castles with my boys.

Whatever age your son is, the truth is that his childhood will pass by quickly. One day he will pack up his car with his iPad and boxes loaded with towels, T-shirts, and jeans and head across the state or country for his college years.

What will you be thinking and feeling at that moment? And how can we make the most of the fleeting, sometimes tiring years of having our sons at home? Someone once said that perhaps parents would enjoy their children more if they stopped to realize the film of childhood can never be run through for a second showing.

Building Relationship

We've talked in earlier chapters about how the foundation of a child's life and development is a close, loving relationship with his parents, especially with his mom in the first years of life. Mothering also includes taking them to doctor's appointments, to birthday parties, to church, sports, and school. It's about helping with homework and sitting in small desks at parent-teacher conferences. It's also about arranging play dates and, years later, waiting for our teen to come home from the junior-senior prom.

But being a mom is about something even more than that. It's about developing a relationship that we hope will last a lifetime with this boy we love. However, connecting and building that relationship isn't always easy.

Psychologist William Pollack says that in much of a boy's growing-up years, "most mothers seem to connect with their sons just being with them, by giving them their undivided attention, and by making themselves available as an unfailing source of love, comfort, and support."[2] When our boys move into elementary school, middle school years to high school, their schedule and ours can become so packed that staying connected is more challenging.

What helps to build that connection is to find something that both you and your son are interested in, enjoy doing, and can share together. Once Edith Schaeffer, author of *What Is a Family?*, shared some wisdom as we talked over a cup of tea: "It's important to be doing something *together*, not just something *for* the child, but something you really enjoy; not just as a reward

93

or a duty, but as having discovered something that can be talked about and shared when you are together."[3]

As a parent, I really wanted to know my sons and daughter. Having lost several close family members at a young age and one of our children, I lived with the sense that life is short. I didn't want to wake up one day after they'd grown up and left and wish we'd spent more time together.

Value the Time

With toddler and preschool sons, there are lots of ways to spend time together, because little ones just enjoy doing simple things with parents—like baking cookies, walking the dog, cuddling up and reading a book, and going to the park or library. Enjoy this brief season when you're the center of their world! Time together (with electronic devices turned off) can also be spent on the floor building a Lincoln Log house, drawing spaceships, throwing a big rubber ball, or playing a board game like Chutes and Ladders or the Go Fish card game.

When our children were young, I went to a lecture by a local child and family psychologist. I was very impacted by the unique "prescription" he gave to parents who came to his office seeking help for a problem with their kids. Any problem. He gave them a daily assignment for either parent to spend at least twenty minutes doing something with the child that the child enjoyed. It didn't matter how you spent it; the important thing was to be consistent with that daily time and not be distracted by the phone, television, or anything else. Giving eye contact, pats or affection, and having interaction while you are playing, building, or doing whatever your child wanted to do. It wasn't something you took away if your child was naughty; it wasn't a reward, but just part of the routine.

This psychologist believed in this focused time together so much that he guaranteed that if parents did this consistently for thirty days and the problem still persisted, he would give them free counseling indefinitely. He had seen it work over and over through the years of his practice. This encouraged me to continue connecting through doing active stuff our boys were interested in as they grew.

Connecting With Preteen and Teenage Sons

Once I met a mother of a twelve-year-old son who bemoaned the fact that he had changed. "He just won't talk to me anymore. He used to tell me about everything but now he's clammed up and will hardly say anything. He doesn't want to be with me." Her son's behavior was pretty normal for his age, as I was reminded when I picked up my grandson Luke today after tennis camp and asked, "How was the camp today? Did you do drills or play actual games?" and all I got was "OK."

I shared with her that children's, and especially boys', emotions and thoughts are a little like oatmeal. If you heat up a pot of oatmeal and it gets hotter and closer to a boil, bubbles come to the surface. In a similar way, as our sons get heated up through doing active things, their thoughts bubble up to the surface. They may even begin to talk. It helps you connect and know what's going on with them, because with boys, action and activity lead to connectivity and bonding.

When I asked what her son enjoyed, she said golf. So she started driving the golf cart for him on afternoons when he played nine holes. She even went to the driving range with her son and took a few golf lessons so she could hit the ball.

Connecting definitely got more challenging when our oldest, Justin, hit adolescence and Chris his preteen years. They didn't want to spend time doing girl things with me like shopping or sitting down at the kitchen table over tea to talk. It was easier to do things with Alison, like looking for earrings at the mall or talking over donuts and hot chocolate after school.

I discovered the best way to connect with my sons was to get on their turf, see what they were interested in doing. Many afternoons after school, after Chris dropped his books on the kitchen table, I asked him, "Wanna shoot some hoops?" Or, depending on the season and weather, play Ping-Pong in the garage, ride bikes, or throw a football. When he was interested in playing golf, I drove the cart for him sometimes.

I had a full-time job as a writer along with being a part-time teacher by this time, but I'd drop what I was doing if Chris or Justin took me up on the offer. Out in the yard we'd go. After a while, they'd share a thought or tell about something that happened at school. Sometimes I'd hear about an exam coming up or a team tryout. But this was a no-strings-attached time together, not for asking a bunch of questions (which was natural for me) or expecting conversation, but just for hanging out.

With Justin, I played lots of tennis games, as that was his main sport and my favorite one. One day in high school when his swing was really strong, he fired a serve over that hit me right in the eye, giving me a shiner. Ouch! Yet in those after-school and Saturday times with the boys, I learned to throw a pretty good spiral football pass and occasionally beat them in Ping-Pong, but my basketball-throwing skills remain pitiful. Chris often chuckled at my underhanded shots.

Sometimes while we played, I heard Justin or Chris tell a story or talk about what was going on with them. Were we able to share that time every day? No, they were too busy, they had sports practice and homework, and I also had a daughter to get to ballet and piano lessons, dinner to fix, and all the regular stuff moms do. But those boys are now grown men in very time-intensive career and family years, and as I look back, it was some of the best times we had together. I cherish the memory of those moments.

Shared time makes regular deposits in your boy's emotional bank account. It might be an interest you both have in reading, music, hiking, bowling, running, or eating homemade cinnamon rolls together on a Saturday morning. Doing a crossword or Sudoko puzzle or going to a movie. Reading and praying together before lights out may be a good connection point when your son is of elementary age, and for some boys, even when they're older. You could teach your son something you know how to do. He might not be interested in learning to play the clarinet, but guitar or drums? It's a possibility for connection.

Have dinner together as a family. Take flashlights for a night stroll with your son around the neighborhood. Get out in nature, and you'll both relax a little. "In a family, anything that is a ritual provides the possibility for emotional 'safety' because it is a familiar niche of time—a protected space—in which there is no pressure to perform, no pressure to measure up, and no threat of judgment," according to Dan Kindlon and Michael Thompson. "If in that shared time together, a parent communicates openness, acceptance, and affection, then a boy learns these values of relationship."[4]

In William Pollack's book *Real Boys*, he confirms the importance of just hanging out and sharing an activity with your son: "A boy's natural language is usually action language,"[5] so the time we spend doing simple, active, enjoyable things with our sons makes a difference.

Connecting Through Music

We may be a generation apart, but music can connect our hearts. Elaine Shaw has found it enriching to learn from her boys, especially in the area of music. Her husband, Guy, was a musician, and music has always been an important part of their lives. Early on, their five boys heard classical music playing in the house and Mom took them to concerts and symphonies. In addition, they were exposed to hymns and beautiful church music. "All the while they were forging their own way," Elaine told me. "They've got this whole universe of music that they've come up with." Though she grew up in a strict Christian family and a narrow life, her sons developed a much more eclectic musical mix of their own.

To connect with her sons and appreciate what they were listening to, Elaine listened to artists she'd never heard of. Bryan was into rap in his adolescent years, so they'd sit and talk about it. In listening and discussing the music with her son, she realized something was being said here, so not to cast it off because the musicians looked different. Although they live in other places, sons Jake, Andrew, and Matthew make her CD mixes of favorite music and call it "A Little Music for Mama" for a Christmas or birthday gift. This is one of the ways she connects with her adult sons.

One of the real blessings for Elaine and her husband has been going to the little church where their oldest son, Trey, was pastor during his furlough year. Trey, his wife, Denise, and their children live in Budapest, Hungary, so it's a thrill to hear him teach there on the rare occasion they get to visit. But during their year in Texas, Elaine played the piano for the small congregation each Sunday and took notes when her son taught God's Word. Just as Elaine did, at different stages of life, when we can see our sons do what they love, participate if invited, or listen to their passion, it helps our connection.

Interactive Ways to Connect With Your Boys (even if they are being "prickly")

Sometimes in adolescence, a young man goes through what I call a "prickly" stage, meaning he is easily angered, offended, or upset—especially by his parents. Sometimes this behavior is just part of the normal pulling away from you in order to become his own person. But keep connected, regardless, and let him know you are always open to discuss things or hang out. He still needs to hear from you and know you care.

It's easy to think when your son pushes you away that he doesn't need you. Your feelings get hurt, so you may withdraw and disconnect. But connections need to continue throughout adolescence. Here are some creative ideas for relationship building:

Leave a note . . . on his pillow, nightstand, or laptop that says, "Let's spend an hour together on Saturday and go to lunch. Your pick." If he doesn't take you up on the offer, don't take it personally. Another time (if he's not talking much) you could leave a message that says, "I'm still proud of you and you'll always be my boy" or "I saw how you were such a good friend to Bill last week. That reminded me of your grandpa, one of the kindest and manliest men I know."

Send a text. Since texting is the language of communication for this generation of young people, send an occasional (rather than five times a day) text like, "I'm thinking of you" or "Good luck on your science test."

Gift giving is a concrete love language most boys appreciate. Think of something your son would like and surprise him: an iTunes card, a new basketball, or a CD of his favorite artist.

Make his favorite dinner. The way to a guy's heart at just about any age is still through his stomach. What are his favorite foods and desserts? Surprise him!

Take him on an errand, if he's fourteen or younger, and drive through Starbucks or stop for a burger or a soft drink. Older sons also might be willing to do this if food is involved. Avoid using this time to lecture or scold. Know when to talk and when to be quiet. And if your son isn't interested in chatting, don't take it personally. (That phrase is becoming a theme in this chapter.)

Let them know you're available. Minnesota mother Cynthia Tonn's approach to connecting with her sons was that if she offered to talk with them about something going on, and they said they weren't interested, she told them where she would be if they changed their minds. Most often, they would come to her and talk about the situation later. Cynthia used her memories of growing up in a dysfunctional home to remind her how hard life is, especially for a young person, and was willing to offer suggestions, acceptance, and encouragement to her sons.

If you've lost your sense of humor, cultivate it. You're going to need it! A son connects better with a mom who has a sense of humor and doesn't take herself, her children, or her family too seriously. He needs a mom who likes to have fun, who laughs at her son's jokes, who sees humor even in his silly ways or adolescent quirkiness. Being able to be a bit lighthearted and occasionally laugh at yourself and your own mistakes and laugh *with* your son (not *at* him) helps release pressure and tension that are present in any family and phase of life, but especially in the adolescent years.

In an office, if the leader of the team is in a bad mood, the employees in her area will catch that mood. When the leader is positive and warm, however, that mood is caught and positively influences the others. The same dynamic exists in families. Humor diffuses stress, helps everyone around you, and lifts your own perspective. Humor can help overcome the drive for perfection and helps you connect with others.

Respect your son. Being respected for who they are and what they think is important for all people, but especially young adults. Respect his right to look or be different, although it may be hard for you. (You may have to give up your desire for others to think well of you.) Respect his ideas and independent opinions even if they are different from yours. Respect his silence and be willing to wait until he asks your advice (even if he rarely does) before you dish it out. See him as the gift that he is *right now* and not someone who needs to be changed. Then you can enjoy the time you do have to connect.

Take a Trip . . . and Let Go of Your Expectations

The summer Chris was about to turn sixteen, I had a trip coming up to California to be a guest on the *Focus on the Family* radio program. Knowing how much he loved major-league baseball and had a dream of playing beach volleyball, I invited him to join me and fly to Los Angeles. I had visions of mother and son chatting on the flight and having some great heart-to-heart moments on the journey. But not so! Good thing I brought an interesting novel.

Chris is a man of few words and was a very quiet teenager, at least with his mom. Nevertheless, we had a memorable time going to see the Dodgers play ball (another of his dreams), went to Universal Studios together, and we talked as we walked down Laguna Beach. He did get to see and play beach volleyball and was happy about that.

One thing I learned in raising and traveling with boys is to be comfortable with some silences and not having to fill the empty space with words. (I had a tendency to do this, so it took time.) And remember before you go, release your expectations and agenda of how you imagine a trip or outing to be with your son. Just let him be who he is and enjoy the moments together, even if it's very quiet.

If a trip isn't possible (or even if it is), take your son on a weekly or monthly date, just the two of you, for a relationship-building evening together. You can go to a favorite restaurant; if he's younger, give him some practice in table manners and encourage him to be gentlemanly and open the door for you. Let him order his food, and besides the time waiting for the food and eating together, there will be chances to communicate on the way to and from the restaurant.

Broaden Your Perspective

Try to keep in mind the long-term goals of parenting: to raise a responsible, healthy, and capable adult male who will one day leave you to be on his own. If your aim also includes building a relationship that lasts a lifetime (i.e., by the time he's grown up, you'll be adult friends), you won't let seasons of prickly, surly, or difficult behavior derail the connection entirely. You've got to keep the big picture and avoid ultimatums that break the relationship, like "You keep doing this and you're out of here" or "It's my way or the highway."

Prickly doesn't necessarily mean prodigal or rebellious, but certain behaviors need to be addressed, especially if they are destructive, addictive, or dangerous. Increased angry outbursts and aggression, interest in drugs and alcohol, and serious depression and withdrawal from family and friends are all signs that need attention. Getting help from a counselor or pastor or an intervention and treatment may be needed if there is an addiction or serious issue persisting. The most unhelpful thing we can do is stay in denial about problems. But your son still needs your support, unconditional love, communication, and prayers.

Avoid overreacting to hurt—even though rejection can feel painful—and accept where your son is for this season, knowing that *"This too will pass."*

Consider examining *yourself* if the prickliness and distance continues: Are you trying to be in his business too much? Are you not letting him be a man? Are you harping on his behavior or appearance? If so, he'll get the message "What is most important in our relationship is for me not to embarrass Mom" and distance himself even more.

If you're feeling very disconnected from your son, one of the best things to do is attempt an honest conversation with him. Psychologist Ken Wilgus advises,

> Let the conversation center around the fact that you miss knowing what's going on with your boy. Ask if there are things you could change that might make it easier for him to share with you. Let him know that when he wants to talk about something, you're available to listen. Above all, remember that simply asking for better communication can be reassuring to him that you're not trying to make him talk.

Many teen boys won't know how to answer questions right away, but given some time, might be encouraged to give you some feedback.

Questions to Ponder, Journal, or Discuss

1. When you and your son spend time together, what are your expectations and hopes?

2. What activities does he like to do best?

3. Is there some common ground you and your son have or could develop—something that you could spend shared time doing?

4. What have been some of you and your son's best times together, either when he was younger or recently?

5. How have you handled a time when your son was "prickly"? Is there a way you've found to stay connected during those times?

6. What do you love and enjoy most about your son right now?

8

A Mom Who Understands Her Son's Unique Personality

Understanding is the beginning of positive influence. A mother's desire to understand her son can equip her with the power to influence his life for good, thereby influencing his family, and his family's family, and all the generations to come.[1]

—John and Helen Burns

Am I doing something wrong? I wondered when our first son was very young.

I loved him dearly. Yet he wasn't anything like my friends' babies—"easy," placid, perpetually happy, sitting contentedly in their car seats during two hours of errands. Compliant and laid back? That was not our son Justin's style. He protested about being confined and needed lots of movement and action. Since he was happiest outdoors, I wore out two strollers walking him hundreds of miles during his first two years.

While he was often exuberant and comfortable in familiar surroundings, he was sometimes fussy in new situations, like our first mother-baby swim class. He grew out of this, though, and was more and more comfortable and outgoing at new places. By fourth grade he was the one who made a friend in the first ten minutes of being at summer camp. His emotions were intense, he was determined to accomplish his goals, and he definitely was spirited. And oh, was he darling with his blond hair and blue eyes!

At the time, as a new mother I thought surely I wasn't doing something right and if I parented like the other moms in the playgroup, maybe my son would be as compliant as theirs. (One mom indicated that would be the case.) I was falling into the trap that afflicts some mothers: comparing our parenting or our children to others.

I realized, however, that because each of our children is a unique creation, unlike any other person on earth, it helps to understand their unique temperament, personality, and bent.

While looking for wisdom, I searched the library and bookstores until I found an insightful resource entitled *Know Your Child* by two child psychiatrists, Drs. Stella Chess and Alexander Thomas.[2] The book was based on a thirty-year clinical study that followed children from birth to adulthood. Chess and Thomas explained that from infancy onward, children vary in their behavior and reactions to stimuli. The temperamental differences aren't random but can be categorized into specific traits, all of which we will look at in this chapter.[3]

- activity level
- rhythm and predictability
- withdrawal or approach to new situations
- adaptability

- sensory threshold
- quality of mood
- intensity of reaction
- distractibility or attention span

This book was a very helpful resource, and as I studied these traits, I began to realize that some of the puzzling things I was experiencing were related to temperament.

As I better understood how our son was wired personality-wise, I was more accepting of his colorful emotions and passionate nature. I also became more confident as a mother. I began to celebrate his lively boy-energy and find more outdoor activities to channel that energy and love for climbing. His persistence and determination meant I needed to choose my battles, deciding the majors, like safety issues, that I needed to stick to, and some of the minors to let go of. I also began to see his great persistence and strong will as a real strength that would serve him well as he got older and faced obstacles. I found ways to encourage his temperament and adjust my behavior to have a better mother-son fit.

Over the years, I've grown to appreciate even more how Justin's qualities are a vital part of his personality. His determined, persevering nature enabled him to earn fifteen business awards during the first year and a half of working for a medical corporation and to continue to gain awards along his career path.

Still energetic and active, he is a runner and tennis player. His excellent people skills contribute to how well he manages, trains, and leads employees in the workplace. With strong verbal skills, he's an effective and articulate communicator, and his enthusiasm for projects and goals is contagious. Justin is a passionate person, who has channeled his personality traits into success and fulfillment in his adult life.

What does this have to do with you and your son? When you're tuned in to his temperament, you'll understand his needs better. As Dan Kindlon and Michael Thompson wrote, "How successful a mother is in seeing her son *only for who he is* . . . has a great deal to do with how successful she is going to be in reading, adapting to, and especially enjoying her son."[4]

It's the match or mismatch that matters in the relationship and how we respond to our child. As Dr. Jane Healy, author of *Your Child's Growing Mind*, says, "We now recognize that the child's personality and response style help determine the way he gets treated by those around him. . . . His behavior may increase the stress, and thus affect the response, of the adults in his life."[5]

Understanding our son's personality takes patience and observation, and a shifting of focus from self and perfection as a mother to learning who God has designed our boy to be. When we do, we can raise him "in keeping with his individual gift or bent" (Proverbs 22:6 AMP) and that leads to *acceptance* rather than disapproval. For example, if you are a fast-moving, talkative mom, you may get impatient with your low-key, silent son who has two speeds—slow and slower. Or if you're a mom who expects your low-adaptability kid to quickly adjust and master new situations, your son will feel a sense of failure because he can't meet your expectations and senses your disappointment.

When we overreact or shame our sons for a personality trait or what we see as a shortcoming, it never leads to true behavior change, but rather shuts them down and teaches them to be ashamed of who they are. It's our job as mothers to understand, accept, and appreciate their individual ways of responding and learning and not try to change them.

Here's what Chris told me recently: "Mom, you recognized and accepted that I've been a pretty independent person all my life and wanted to do things by myself even when I was small.

There's certainly an art to letting your child feel independent and allowing that to develop into a good sense of independence for the long haul. You didn't make me feel dependent by responding, 'No, you have to do it my way' or 'I'll do that for you,' but you let me figure it out." Chris now has a darling six-year-old daughter, Lucy, who is very independent like her dad. Since Lucy was very tiny she's said, "I'll do it *myself*!"

As a child, Chris was an introvert—quiet, reserved, and didn't need a lot of talk—and he still is as an adult. For a relational person like me who (as he said) sometimes tried to draw out more conversation than he wanted, I had a lot to learn from his thoughtful, reflective nature. And I've learned to appreciate quiet people and listen attentively when they have something to say. After all, Proverbs says that a man of few words is wise.

Harville Hendrix and Helen Hunt wrote in *Giving the Love That Heals: A Guide for Parents*, "One of the most challenging life-tasks of any parent is to experience oneness with a newborn and then to gradually help this infant grow into a person who is *not* the parent—to see the ways the child is different and to honor them not only by allowing differences but by genuinely appreciating them."[6]

Chris was serious, studious, and from age nine or ten focused on becoming a doctor. Today he is a dermatologist who was awarded "Top Five Navy Doctors" in the nation by the surgeon general of the U.S. Navy.

Temperament Traits

Understanding all three of our children's unique temperaments freed me to accept and celebrate their personalities and enjoy them instead of trying to change them. We need to see our child for the gift that he is now and not as someone who needs to be changed. That's why I want to share with you what I learned about the differences and qualities in children's temperaments.

Let me encourage you to become a student of your son, especially in the early years—because the strongest emotional stimulation needed for good brain development is *attunement*. That means being "tuned in" to your son's cues and clues, noticing his moods, understanding what's going on, and responding in a way that fosters emotional and mental growth. Understanding temperament traits is a great way to start. Here they are:

- **Activity level** means the proportion of active and inactive periods. Some little boys prefer less active pastimes like drawing, watching TV, building, or reading for long stretches of time, while others are turbocharged and choose active play like running, climbing, riding a bike, or throwing a ball against a wall or garage. They may watch TV for a short while, but jump up after ten minutes to move.

- **Predictability and consistency.** Some babies are full of surprises: there is no regularity to their hunger, sleeping, and waking. Others are very predictable. They wake up at the same time each day, get hungry at regular times, and go potty at the same time every day like clockwork. If you're trying to get the unpredictable baby on a schedule and keep him there, you may feel some days like you're hitting your head against the wall. It's not that he's a bad child, just that you may need to be more flexible and tuned in to his needs.

- **Intensity of emotions and reactions** means how kids respond to frustration and express their feelings. A high-intensity child may laugh enthusiastically when he is happy, cry loudly or lose his temper in a big way when angry. It's easy to read how this boy is feeling. A low-intensity child, however, is more laid back and quiet about expressing his emotions and needs. He may show he's happy about something with a little smile or not even tell you when he's hurt. Listening and staying tuned in is vital so you don't ignore his needs.

If a baby's or young child's subtle expressions of emotion, especially pain or distress, are not taken seriously and responded to, physical symptoms can arise. Not only can a medical situation get worse, but emotional and mental growth can be stifled.[7]

Our first- and second-born sons are good examples: Justin was more high-intensity and verbally expressive, whereas Chris was lower-intensity and quieter about expressing his feelings and needs. The first time my mother held Chris, she said, "Cheri, you need to pay attention to this baby, because he's so easygoing; his big brother is likely to be the one who commands your focus." Mama had raised six children and she was right on target.

- **Positive or negative mood: pleasant and joyful or negative and often unhappy.** Our children had fairly positive moods in early childhood unless they were sick. Chris, however, had the most consistently positive mood of all. He woke up happy and went to bed with a smile on his cute little face. He rarely cried unless something was wrong and was usually content to play, observe, and participate in whatever was happening around him. Kids are always developing and changing. Those with a negative mood often fuss for no reason after waking up and later see the glass as "half empty" in school or friend situations. They can grow more optimistic and positive with help and understanding.

- **Flexibility and adaptability** means how slowly or rapidly a child adjusts to changes to a new routine, school, or situation. Some kids are naturally resistant to change. In a new class or school, they're shy, hold back, and watch until they can relax enough to be themselves or move into the group. Others jump in and make a new friend five minutes after arriving.

- **Easily distracted or very focused.** *Focused* means keeping at a task even if interrupted, while *distractible* means being easily drawn away. What a valuable trait focus is! There's a saying that *the successful person is the average person, focused*. But if you're trying to get your hyper-focused son to stop his Lego project and leave for the doctor's office without advance warning, it may not seem like a strength.

- Related to the above traits are **attention span and persistence level.** A boy with low persistence begins his math problems, but if he gets frustrated with the first few, he tends to give up. A boy with high persistence keeps trying, even when it's very difficult. He will doggedly persevere until the assignment is done. Although many students, especially boys, are diagnosed with Attention Deficit Disorder today, which can be due to a neurological issue, researchers Chess and Thomas found the length of attention span is also related to temperament.[8] Some kids are simply more task oriented and persistent in their endeavors.

- **Sensory threshold** means how disturbed or oblivious kids are to external noises, textures, lights, and changes in their home or environment. A child with a low sensory threshold is noise sensitive. He can also be the one who can't concentrate when the tag on the inside of his T-shirt is scratching his back, or the one who needs lower light to do his best in the classroom.

The Tale of Two Brothers

Wouldn't it be a bit boring if all the children in one family were just the same? I like this quote from Marcelene Cox: "Children in a family are like flowers in a bouquet: there's always one determined to face in an opposite direction from the way the arranger desires."[9]

In one Texas family I know, there is a variety of temperaments, starting with the oldest two boys. The firstborn son, Isaac, has always been bright and detail oriented. He is a rule follower and wants his siblings to follow rules too. He's the "policeman" who can annoy the other children with his bossiness. Also, with a lower activity level than the other siblings, Isaac likes to sit and read, think, make things, or build Legos rather than run in the yard with his younger brother, Noah. Isaac is as cautious and reflective as Noah is adventurous and energetic.

When he begins a task or project, Isaac is persistent and focused, often not stopping for a snack or a break until he's finished. When he received an excavation kit as a gift, he worked and hammered in the sand all day until he retrieved the pretend skull of a dinosaur. Noah was excited to help hammer at first, but got diverted, and after a few minutes, just played in the sand. Isaac is predictable and likes everything to be structured and scheduled.

Noah is more unpredictable, moody, and sensitive; Isaac is more reserved in his emotions. Independent Noah likes to do things on his terms and in his way. He's better at athletics and loves to be active outdoors. Yet these are both wonderful boys, and as their personalities have developed and had room to grow in their family, they are becoming outstanding young men with their own temperament styles, interests, and gifts.

A Marvelous Mix

The mixture of temperament traits are a big part of what makes up personality. Keep in mind, though, that the issue is not that a child's personality is good or bad. It's not whether your son is difficult or easy. A more important question would be *Is your son's temperament and yours a good fit? Do you understand him or misread his behavior?* How children do in the long run has more to do with the temperament match (or mismatch) between mother and son than it does with your child having a certain "ideal" personality, because this fit affects the bonding and relationship you have.

I've seen mothers of very active boys who called them un-disciplined or disobedient because they don't sit still enough to please them. Other moms criticize their sons for not having enough tenacity to get their homework done, when the problem may be low persistence and high distractibility.

A mother with an unhappy, negative child who withdraws from the other students in kindergarten class may feel it's her fault even though she's a loving, positive mother. Or she may push her son to be friendlier and adapt faster than he is able at his particular stage of development. Mothers are frequently annoyed at their sons who don't want to leave their video game to eat dinner, not realizing that their very perseverance to finish the game is a valuable trait. In each of these cases, continual misunderstanding and friction produces stress in the mom and resentment toward her in the son.

Although how we parent and the environment kids live in do have an influence, a great part of children's personalities are pre-wired and not caused by something we did, as Chess and Thomas's study shows. We're not that powerful! God is their Creator and He made each child uniquely, wonderfully, and marvelously, with a bright future in mind for them.[10]

Part of our role as parents is teaching our kids the impor-tance of accepting our differences, which helps us learn how to work together in the family, at school, and at work. As family counselors David and Jan Stoop say, "We begin to do this by accepting the differences we see in our children and learning how to understand and affirm them in these areas."[11]

What we can do as mothers is to be flexible and *celebrate the differences of temperament, particularly your own child's*—all the while being aware that what appears to be a negative char-acteristic in a boy may become his greatest strength. If you have a very energetic, active son, but you have a low activity level, you may feel wiped out at the end of the day just trying to keep up with him. Sometimes you may be irritated when you want him to slow down, but it's only eight PM and he still has plenty of energy.

Have hope! As an adult this same son may have tremendous physical and mental energy, which when pointed in the right direction will make him very productive. The boy with a melancholy mood may have an artistic bent to write or paint great works. The sensitive son with intense emotions may become a successful actor, musician, or psychologist.

Traits and even talents in children often appear in a less than ideal package. For example, bossy kids can be frustrating to deal with. But the dominant son, who tells everyone what to do and won't stop until they do, actually may have a budding administrative bent and persistent determination that will equip him later to become the CEO of a company. Argumentative kids who challenge everything we say and are always asking *why?* show a bent toward the analytical talent that engineers possess. Because this and other traits can be very frustrating, we need eyes of faith to see the positive potential within them.

We'll look at different learning styles in the next chapter and how you can recognize them. But remember that sometimes your child needs time to grow into his big, unique personality, and it takes patience on your part. Sometimes the best parts of your son may be hidden from you because of your own stress or family environment, or his immaturity. Accept and understand your son (strengths, weaknesses, difficult or easy temperament), pray for him, be his greatest encourager—and most of all, enjoy him, for the fingerprints he leaves on the wall are going to get higher and higher, and one day they will disappear. Then watch as his future unfolds before your eyes.

Questions to Ponder, Journal, or Discuss

1. What are some of your favorite aspects of your son's temperament and personality?

2. What is a more challenging trait of his temperament?

3. Is there a difficult temperament trait that you already see becoming a strength or you've realized how it can be an asset as he grows up? What is it?

4. How is the match or "fit" between you and your son's personality? Is it improving? What ways can you better accept or embrace him as he is?

5. Spend some time in prayer, asking God to help you see your son with eyes of faith, and what he can become when he grows into his personality and gifts. Jot down what you learn.

9

A Mom Who Helps Her Son Shine in School and Beyond

As young people look for their talents, all they need is the smallest sign of God-given ability. No matter how underdeveloped, a gift given back to God will be more than enough. Adults can help by looking for the smallest potential and foreseeing how God can turn it into something wonderful.[1]

—Miles McPherson, *The Power of Believing in Your Child*

The six-year-old boy dragged himself through the door, dropped his backpack, and looked up at his mother with a discouraged frown.

"How was your day?" she asked, setting some graham crackers and milk in front of him. Normally talkative, he muttered "okay," munched his snack, and then flopped down in front of the TV.

117

This wasn't the first difficult school day. Although this boy tried his best, his teacher had written nothing but negative comments on his progress reports, such as "needs to work faster" and "needs improvement in math skills" but wasn't willing to give him extra help. That only added to his discouragement.

Has your son at one time or another faced struggles at school? Perhaps he has a learning difference, or just doesn't shine in the classroom like he does on the baseball or soccer field. Unfortunately, it's easy to get caught up in the negative labels placed on kids today, particularly boys: underachiever, learning disabled, oppositional disorder. (When I was in school, this was considered a stubborn or misbehaving kid, not a psychological disorder.)

Throughout the years that I taught school, I saw over and over that negative labels create a downward spiral. Low expectations lead to less effort from the student, which results in less achievement. A better strategy than negative labeling is to determine what the problem area is that is blocking learning, get evaluation at a local university's education department, and make a plan of action that includes compensating strategies.

Thankfully, the reverse of negative labeling is also true. When parents have high but realistic expectations and provide support, structure, and strategies to compensate for weaknesses, great things can happen in a boy's life. Curtis Pride, a longtime major-league baseball player, is a good example. Despite a 95 percent hearing loss, Curtis never let his disability deter him from pursuing his dreams. His parents told him that with hard work, he could do anything—and they educated themselves on how to create an environment that would enable him to succeed academically and socially.

Through years of speech therapy, Curtis learned oral communication, and his parents mainstreamed him from seventh grade on—against the experts' recommendations. Curtis became a top-notch academic student and gifted athlete who went on to make it in the professional ranks.

Every person has the potential to do something better than thousands of other people. What makes the difference in the late bloomer who blooms and the underachiever who achieves is often the mother who doesn't give up on him, who believes in him, and who helps her son find his God-given gifts.

Something as simple as structure can make a big difference in a boy's life. The structure that Dr. Benjamin Carson's mother provided helped him move from being a troubled student in the lowest reading group in second grade to being at the top of his class within a year. The family was poor, and since their father had abandoned the family, Ben's mother worked three jobs to support her two children. Even though she couldn't read, she figured out a way to help her son achieve. When Ben saw a slide show of a medical missionary at church, a spark was ignited within him. He decided he wanted to be a doctor and help people around the world.

After sharing his goal with his mother, she didn't discourage this seemingly impossible dream. She believed in him, yet provided some firm guidelines: No television was allowed until all his homework was finished; every week he had to read *at least two books* in addition to those required for school, with book reports handed in to her. In time, Ben went to the top of his class and stayed there until he graduated, attended Yale University on scholarship, and Johns Hopkins School of Medicine. He became and remains one of the top pediatric neurosurgeons in the world, who has given hundreds of children a second chance at life.[2]

In the parenting and women's conferences I've conducted through the years, I've met many moms who are frustrated and bewildered because the bright, curious, happy son they used to know has shut down to learning, is negative about school, or underachieves. A great way to turn this around or prevent it is to understand your son's learning style—which means the patterns of strengths and weaknesses that make up the way he processes and learns information. While no two people learn alike, there are some learning styles that are particular to, and most often seen in, boys.

How Boys Think and Process Information

In the early years, boys tend to be kinesthetic learners, or what I call movers and doers. They learn best when they can use movement, like going from one learning center to another with different activities that build on the same concept. This is important not only in kindergarten but also in fifth grade and higher. Some of the best schools are using this method. Boys need to get their muscles and/or touch involved in learning by doing experiments, rehearsing, role playing, making volcanoes, inventing, all the while taking an active approach as much as possible.

When they can count actual pennies, nickels, dimes, and quarters instead of looking at coins on a worksheet to add them up, they understand money better. When they can trace letters in a big sand tray, they remember them more readily. At home, they can stay focused on practicing spelling words or math facts (with more facts going into their long-term memories) while shooting Nerf basketballs into a basket mounted on a door, instead of sitting in a chair.

In elementary school, most boys tend to continue to favor kinesthetic learning for certain subjects (science, math) and visual-spatial learning comes to the forefront. According to therapists Stephen James and David Thomas,

Boys, in general, are wired to be visually stimulated. Sixty-seven percent of boys are visual learners, meaning they absorb information from illustrations, symbols, photos, icons, diagrams, graphs, and other visual models. Another way of saying this is that a boy's brain turns on when he sees words, whereas a girl's brain responds more readily to hearing words. . . . If instructions are simply spoken, there's always the chance they'll fly in one ear and out the other.[3]

It doesn't mean that there aren't boys who are auditory-verbal learners with language talent. Those kids learn best by hearing explanations and talking or discussing the information. The fact is, more girls learn verbally, especially in early childhood and elementary school.

Some children respond to a combination of learning styles and need to mix methods to reach their potential. And all students benefit from doing hands-on learning activities, like doing an electricity experiment instead of just reading about the subject in a book. Handling small animal bones when they study the skeleton and making learning centers on subjects of interest, like constellations, spiders, dolphins, and aerospace, motivates learning. Doing reams of worksheets does not. And instead of looking at a diagram of a flower in a book, dissecting a flower on a white sheet of paper and labeling the parts will teach them much more.

Concrete projects such as these are not just for younger students. In graduate school, much of the learning takes place in labs, so much higher level thinking and discovery can take place through kinesthetic projects.

Also, if at home you provide the raw materials of creativity, such as paint, modeling clay, Popsicle sticks, giant cardboard boxes to make forts and hideouts, large rolls of butcher paper, canvas, and paintbrushes, they can exercise their imagination and create art. With old game pieces like checkers, dice, spinners, poker chips, and cardboard, they can make up new games. If boys have a work space and the raw materials of invention like duct tape, rubber bands, cardboard boxes, hammers, screwdrivers, flashlights, old toys and clocks or other things they can take apart—they can tinker, build things, develop their ideas, and just have fun.

Be sure your son gets enough exercise. Sitting all day in school chairs can be challenging, and coming home to several hours of video/computer games and television is not the best for his learning. James and Thomas report, "We know that boys want their MTV, PS3, Wii, DSL, and Xbox 360, but these kinds of media are bad news for their brains. There's clear evidence that the more visual media a boy takes in, the worse off his sleep, learning, and memory will be."[4]

Instead, have your son run around the perimeter of the house, shoot baskets outside, or jump on a trampoline after school before starting homework. When he's fidgety or frustrated with an assignment and has spent fifteen to twenty minutes on it, suggest a break for movement: a brief walk around the block or some other activity before he returns to finish his homework.

Ride bikes together. Get your son involved in team sports like soccer or basketball that build friendships with other boys and find the "sweet spot" in athletics or another activity he wants to pursue. All of these provide good "wiggle time" and help his brain work to its optimum.

Bringing Out the Best

Discovering your son's learning style and strengths is a key to achievement in school and helps all children become more aware of their talents. It's not a formula or panacea for all learning problems, but a way of finding active strategies to study that coordinate with how their brain works. In the process, you'll know how to better equip your son and eliminate homework stress. If you want to help your son shine, try the following four strategies.

Build on his strengths. Instead of focusing on negative labels, ask, What are my son's strengths? For which weaknesses does he need help to compensate? Then develop an action plan—and implement it.

What made the most difference with our sons was uncovering their true talents: For Justin, communication skills, focus, people smarts, contagious enthusiasm, determination to overcome obstacles, and a creative way of synthesizing ideas to come up with new ones. With Chris, his analytical thinking, spatial and visual memory, his focus, curiosity, and desire for facts (he read the *World Book Encyclopedia* for hours once he learned to read). While we encouraged both in their assignments, we also helped them learn to capitalize on their strengths. We wanted our boys to see that "school smarts" and "test smarts" are only part of the picture.

It wasn't all smooth sailing, of course. For Justin, math and science continued to be challenging. But we encouraged him to look for subjects that sparked his interests. By his junior year of high school, he'd found them: English, writing, business, and history. He profited from getting to shadow some businessmen in their work and assist an attorney, along with a variety of other jobs in the summer.

I showed Justin how to tap into his verbal strengths and strengthen memory by using a tape recorder and blank cassette tape as a study aid. When he had to memorize a long Shakespeare passage, he recorded it on the tape. Then he practiced by saying the lines of the play along with the recording as he drove

123

to high school tennis practice or his part-time job after school. By doing this for several days, he was able to say the passage letter-perfect in front of the class and receive an A.

Chris liked to study alone. But Justin held study groups at our house, where he and the other guys would hash over the key issues of a chapter, try to outguess the teacher on test questions, or take a practice test they'd created. He continued studying this way through college. Eventually he began getting A's in English and history, and the momentum and confidence he developed helped him to put out more effort in his tougher courses.

Having high expectations for your son doesn't mean pushing, taking control, or doing his assignments or projects for him. On the contrary, it means empowering him by sharing study skills that work for his learning style. For more depth on this subject and strategies for each learning style, read my book *Talkers, Watchers, and Doers: Unlocking Your Child's Unique Learning Style* (NavPress).

Break tasks down into doable bites, whether for school or home assignments. A short list of tasks to be completed on a bright index card works better than reeling off a list of ten things he needs to do to clean his room and tackle chores. It will also increase his ability to finish the list.

Get help from someone else. Sometimes finding another person to help your son study for tests is a great boost to a boy who is struggling in school—especially if he's tired of Mom's involvement in his homework.

When Margaret's son, Brad, was a third grader in a private school, he received an F in math and low grades in reading, despite lots of effort. The school wanted to drop him into a lower-level class. His mom knew Brad was bright, so she hired a bright young man in the neighborhood to be Brad's "study buddy" and tutor once a week. They also had Brad tested by a local university education professor to determine the specific areas where he needed help, and found a local school where he could get individualized teaching in those areas for the next year. Margaret had high hopes for Brad, and convinced the teacher to give him another chance.

Margaret knew Brad could set goals and work doggedly to achieve them. What others saw as stubbornness, she saw as one of God's gifts—and shared that with him. "God has given you the ability to take what looks negative, Brad, and turn it into a positive. Your determination will take you a long way," she encouraged him. Although Brad didn't test well at a young age, his perseverance helped him press on when things were difficult. While he had to work hard at his studies, often harder than fellow classmates for the same grade, he earned a bachelor's degree in psychology and a PhD in industrial psychology—and was on his way to a fulfilling career.

Never write your son off academically or allow others to. Lack of early success does not spell out a boy's future. Some men who have achieved the most as adults gained their drive from the struggles they faced when they were young. John Sabolich, one of the top prosthetics designers in the world, struggled as a young student. Because of his innovation and technical ability, amputees throughout the United States and the world can jump, dance, be cheerleaders, compete in races, skydive, and live normal lives.

But it didn't look like John would do anything significant when he failed every year in school until seventh grade. At that point, John was so discouraged about the straight-F report card he'd received that he catapulted into high gear. He hired a tutor (a retired teacher) who worked with him weekly, helping him catch up in reading, math, and other subjects. She didn't write him off like his teachers had. He became the hardest worker in his class and attended New York University to study prosthetics and orthotics.

Everything came late for John, even sports ability and finding out what his talents were. But he discovered he was good at remembering diagrams and pictures, not abstract words. Classroom instruction was mainly about lectures and words. He had great dexterity in his hands and a bent toward problem-solving, three-dimensional thinking, and design. As he applied these strengths to the classroom by finding the most efficient ways to study—highlighting important passages in various colors, taking quick notes, and making his own diagrams to illustrate concepts—he excelled.

Do you have a late-blooming son or one who is just not achieving in the traditional pencil-and-paper-focused classroom? Don't automatically think he is learning disabled. Is a fox disabled because his hearing is so sharp he can hear a sound twenty miles away and yet cannot fly? Like John Sabolich, Thomas Edison, Winston Churchill, and Albert Einstein, there are many boys who have had learning differences that caused struggles in school, yet out of those very differences emerged the talents, intelligence, and eventually the skills that enabled them to succeed.

Let me encourage you, Mom, not to lose heart. There are doctors and bestselling authors, Oscar-winning actors, CEOs, prime ministers, presidents, and countless men who have contributed much to humanity by using their skills and gifts and finding ways to overcome their challenges. Have high expectations for your son, be a student of him so you can discover his strengths and "center of learning excitement" (what he's most interested in and wants to learn about), and show him ways to use his strengths to study and achieve his best.

A Boy's Brain

It's helpful to understand some of the ways boys and girls are different in learning and brain development. When I taught school, I often observed a sharp difference in the verbal skills of girl students compared to boys in the sixth, seventh, and eighth grades. By the ninth grade, some boys were beginning to catch up, but still were behind the girls in language skills until their senior year of high school or even into their freshman year of college, where I taught English for several years.

There were other differences. The girls followed oral directions more quickly and had their hands up to answer questions faster than the boys. Because their fine motor skills are superior to boys' during the elementary years, pencil-and-paper/worksheet activities are easier for girls. The boys had a harder time sitting still, especially on rainy days when they couldn't go outside. Most of the girls easily contained their energy until recess. Although there are certainly exceptions, many boys have some unique challenges in school—even though they may be bright and capable.

Part of the reason has to do with brain development. Researchers have found that the "frontal lobe, a part of the brain crucial to general learning and to impulse control, grows later in the majority of males and is more vulnerable to disruptions in infant and toddler development in the male brain than in the female."[5] In certain cognitive learning, boys lag behind girls, not because they lack high intelligence, but because their brains develop differently.

That's why, as Dan Kindlon and Michael Thompson write in *Raising Cain*,

> Grade school is largely a feminine environment, populated predominantly by women teachers and authority figures, that seems

127

rigged against boys, against the higher activity level and lower level of impulse control that is normal for boys. . . . In this setting a boy's experience of school is as a thorn among roses; he is a different, lesser, and sometimes frowned-upon presence, and he knows it.[6]

Here are some helpful facts to know from Michael Gurian's book *The Minds of Boys*:

- Males are diagnosed with the majority of brain disorders in schools, mostly ADD/ADHD (seven boys for every one girl).
- Over two-thirds of children labeled learning-disabled and 90 percent of children labeled behaviorally disabled are boys.
- Boys have a more fragile biology and are more vulnerable to psychiatric diseases and learning disorders.[7]

There are also far more boys than girls taking Ritalin and other attention-deficit medication. Yet there are plenty of assets and strengths that boys bring to the classroom. Many possess a strong pragmatism and problem-solving ability if they are given a chance to use them. In addition, Kindlon and Thompson report, "Boys are direct; they act and speak in simple terms. Their more slowly developing language skills are apparent in their often blunt and unsophisticated humor or their preference for action over negotiation. . . . The average boy's gifts are wrapped in high activity, impulsivity, and physicality—boy power—and the value of these gifts depends on the teacher, the boy, and the moment."[8]

It takes creative, patient teachers to motivate boys to learn, to unlock their potential and provide hands-on opportunities and projects instead of stacks of worksheets to complete every day. Boys also need mothers to help find their strengths so they can use them to learn. We all need to work together with schools and teachers for the best outcomes for boys.

I admire the many moms homeschooling today who are dedicated to providing the best environment for their children to learn and cooperate with other homeschooling parents for labs, chemistry, foreign-language study, advanced math, or other subjects they aren't strong in. Many of these home-schooled students have outstanding college and graduate-school achievement levels and find fulfillment and success in career paths.

A Mother's Support

Even a boy with major challenges can achieve much with a mother's support and understanding of his strengths. Valerie's son, Brian, was born with Williams syndrome, a genetic disorder that causes mental retardation, heart problems, and other medical issues. By age eight, Brian hadn't mastered the alphabet or learned to read. Valerie wasn't deterred, she told me. She kept reading to Brian at night. The teachers at his special education school finally told her not to expect much of her son because he just wasn't learning words and putting them together into sentences or gaining the comprehension he needed to learn to read.

However, this mom paid attention and kept looking for Brian's biggest interest and skill. When she realized he was fascinated with the car wash they went through every Saturday, she used that interest to open a world of learning for her son. She put simple words such as *car wash*, *soap*, *enter*, and *exit* on flashcards around the house. After Brian learned those, she asked him to pick a word out of their "car wash" word box and use it in a sentence. Together they compiled his sentences into a book. Within six months, he was able to read his first book ever back to his mom.

As Brian learned more words, his interest in reading took off. He always had stacks of library books by his bedside table and in the family room and enjoyed reading all kinds of genres. His parents had the cleanest car in the neighborhood, and Brian had lots of new friends—car-wash owners from far and wide who'd heard about him and wanted to encourage him.

His love of the car-wash industry culminated a few years later when eleven-year-old Brian was the keynote speaker before the six thousand members of the International Car Wash Association's annual convention. He gave such a dynamic speech he received a standing ovation. This was the first of many conventions he was invited to address. Brian's goal became owning and operating car-wash businesses so he could employ people who had special challenges. And he continued to be an avid reader, though his teachers were sure he'd never learn to read.[9]

God tells us He has plans to give our children a bright hope and a future (Jeremiah 29:11). By communicating positive expectations for your son, building on his strengths, encouraging him, and praying for him, you'll be surprised at—and grateful for—what he can accomplish.

Questions to Ponder, Journal, or Discuss

1. What are your son's strengths, weaknesses, or frustrations related to book or school learning?

2. What are his talents and best areas of "smarts" or intelligence?

3. What is he most interested in that you could build on so that he could master certain academic subjects?

4. What are your expectations for his learning and academic growth? What are his goals and yours?

5. Does your son's learning style or way of processing information allow him opportunities to shine in his present school setting?

10

A Mom Who Develops Her Son's Character

Not gold, but only man can make
A people great and strong;
Men who, for truth and honor's sake
Stand fast and suffer long.
Brave men who work while others sleep,
Who dare while others fly . . .
They build a nation's pillars deep
And lift them to the sky.

—"A Nation's Strength"
by Ralph Waldo Emerson

Throughout history, part of a mother's role has been to shape her son's moral character and instill values. And *moms do shape us*, especially our characters and beliefs. I know my mother did in countless ways: teaching me and my sisters and brother a strong work ethic, kindness, and forgiveness from our very earliest years, through verses like "Be kind to each other, tenderhearted, forgiving . . ." (Ephesians 4:32 NLT). She imparted her values by example and her many sayings, such as "A penny saved is a penny earned," "When God closes a door, He opens a window," and "When things are difficult we should keep trying and never give up."

Mama imparted the value of generosity to us by offering warm hospitality to people far and wide and giving to others. Every Easter when she bought our six pairs of shoes to wear on Easter Sunday, she bought brand-new shoes for six children at the Children's Home as well. That and other generous acts stamped an indelible value of giving to others on my child's heart and each of my siblings'.

Although character curriculum is taught in some schools today, home is still the best place for boys to begin learning ethics and values—and moms are the best teachers because they usually spend the most time with their children. Yes, fathers have a big responsibility to teach their sons solid moral foundations, and we hope they do. But mothers hold a primary role in character building, which can make a lifelong difference. That's because responsibility, kindness, honesty, cooperation, determination, and other values influence how our sons will behave in the classroom, what kind of actions they will show on the athletic field, and how they will conduct themselves in their career, relationships, and eventually their own family.

The importance of shaping our children's character was underscored by Thomas Lickona, professor of education at the State University of New York: "If children are to survive and thrive in this society, it's up to parents to reclaim their authority and instill good values in their children at a very early age."[1]

Although there are universal values like responsibility, respect, service, good work ethic, determination, and stewardship, *faith* tops the list of values that Dr. Lickona says children need most in the twenty-first century.[2] Faith is what gives a boy a sense of worth and purpose and helps him thrive no matter what difficulties he faces.

From the cradle through adolescence, the growing-up years are a golden opportunity to instill values in our sons. It sounds like a big responsibility, but it's not an onerous task! The basic concepts of honesty, perseverance, hospitality, commitment, loyalty, and respect for others can be naturally worked into our everyday family life.

If you get only 1 percent growth in your son's character each week, you'll see 50 percent growth in a year.[3]

Moms naturally engage in the process of character building as they're parenting, loving, wiping tears, feeding, and reading books to their kids. When we teach our boys to play fair, to share, to say thank-you, and to be responsible in doing their chores, we're building their character. When we teach them by example that *people are more important than things* (one of the values that I hope was imparted to our sons and daughter), that they are to respect others and be especially respectful to women, then we are building a foundation for their lives.

As educator Lynda Hunter Bjorklund wrote, "Teaching values can naturally lend itself to nurturing relationships. . . . Classrooms for teaching your children values happen at unexpected and unplanned-for times and places."[4]

Because character and virtues are transferred through daily life, through relationships and family life more effectively than studying a workbook, character building is a slow, day-by-day process. It's not mastered overnight, but by continual modeling, patient instruction, family interaction, and practical application.

We certainly can't depend on the society around us to impart good character to our children! News headlines and CNN are filled with the moral failures of people in government and leader-ship: CEOs serving time for Ponzi schemes and insider trading, professional athletes doping with illegal substances to improve their performances, priests who abuse children, politicians in Washington, DC, who have taken bribes.

Kids are watching, and they are influenced by this moral downslide in our culture and communities. It's one of the reasons there is a crisis of values in our country, particularly in young people. Cheating is at an all-time high. Students wonder why they shouldn't cheat; they don't see a reason. Bullying has always been around, but the incidences of bullying weaker or younger kids has escalated. Drug use and premarital sex are characteristic of the lives of many young people.

Why Building Character Is Important Parenting Work

But even with the cultural downslide all around us, you can make a difference and raise your son to become a man of character. It's well worth the effort to be intentional about this part of parenting.

Boys with strong values and character aren't as vulnerable to peer pressure. They develop more confidence and strength to make a positive difference in the world around them. They are less likely to abuse drugs or alcohol, are more likely to practice abstinence, and are better prepared for the challenges of life. What your son learns from you about being honest, thankful, and kind has a powerful influence. Your consistent example can reinforce these values on a daily basis. When you practice, discuss, and read about these values as part of life together, you'll be fostering your son's growth in morals and character.

There are lots of ways to help your son grow into a man of character. Sometimes it's the small things that stick throughout life. One young man told me, "My mother never used the words 'failure' or 'You won't measure up' with me. Whether it was a calculus class I was struggling with or losing a spot on the varsity team, she always said things like 'Keep trying,' 'Learn from your mistakes,' 'You're never a failure until you give up,' 'Losing a battle doesn't mean you've lost the war.' I've never forgotten them."

What Are *Your* Core Values?

Values means whatever we judge worth . . .

- *Being* (like happy, committed, honest, or successful)
- *Doing* (like working hard, helping others, or reading)
- *Having* (like money, peace, or close family relationships)

The first step in building character is to *decide what core or central values* you want your son to understand and live out as he grows. A good place to look when you're considering important values is the Bible. Absolutes are given in the Ten Commandments, which, contrary to modern opinion, are not titled the "Ten Suggestions." Also, the teachings of Jesus in the Gospels and passages like Galatians 5:22–23 (which lists the fruits of the Spirit: love, joy, peace, patience, kindness, goodness, gentleness, faithfulness, and self-control) provide guidance. Another great place in the Bible for values is the book of Proverbs, which is full of descriptions of positive and negative character traits and the consequences of each.

After some reflection and reading, write down the five to eight core values you want to help your son integrate into his life, with space in between them. Then as you gain ideas from this book and other sources, jot down practical ideas or activities on how to impart those core values.

Gentlemanly Character

It is important to teach your son not to talk down to or verbally abuse a girl (sister, friend) or woman, especially his mother. This needs to be the one "line in the sand" boundary a mom should be vigilant about. Men who grow up to put women down make very poor husbands and fathers, businessmen, and co-workers.

You can also teach your son gentlemanly manners—which girls like in a man—and allow him to practice when you're out together, such as to a restaurant:

- Opening the door for you and letting you go first
- Standing up when a lady comes into the room
- How to address various women they come in contact with
- Letting the girl or woman order first in a restaurant
- Giving up their seat on the subway, bus, or train for a girl or woman
- Expressing thanks and saying "I'm sorry" when needed

Actions Speak Louder Than Words

Did you know that because kids learn best by imitation, your example as a *role model* is the most persuasive, positive tool you have to impart values? For example, if you want your son to stay on the soccer team even though they've lost every game so far, let him see you sticking with a difficult project at work or at home. Then when you say, "I know your soccer team's had a rough season but that's no reason to miss games or quit. Hang in there," your words will have more impact. If you want him not to make excuses or avoid dishonesty, don't call in sick at your place of work when you are simply tired and want the day off.

Children are always watching the adults around them—in the car, at the dinner table, in front of the TV, standing in a long line at the grocery store or the mall. These behind-the-scenes times are where kids learn the most because good character is better caught than taught.

A mom's behavior communicates a great deal about what is important to her, and her children tend to follow in her footsteps. Most of the time they do what we do rather than what we say.

Let them see you choose honesty and forgiveness; let them hear you acknowledge your mistakes so they know you're human. Show them the value of admitting you were wrong when you've blown it.

Gratefulness is a value your kids can learn in an enjoyable way by putting a small "blessing basket" in the middle of the dinner table with small slips of paper inside. Family members jot down things they're thankful for and put them in the basket. Each evening, or once a week, these are read aloud. Thanking God for blessings small and great while driving your son to school or doing errands is a good way to stir up a grateful heart.

Getting your son involved in a community service or ministry you're doing helps pass on the intangible but important value of serving others. For our family, Project Angel Tree's Christmas ministry to prisoners' children was something we did for several years. We took our sons and daughter with us to pick out special gifts and deliver them to the children. Our kids shopped with us for the food that made up Thanksgiving and Christmas dinner baskets that we delivered together to families in need.

Justin and Tiffany, our son and daughter-in-law, take Caleb and Caitlin to the City Rescue Mission to serve evening meals several times a year. The kids set up and ran lemonade stands to make money to send to a family that lost two children and their home in a tornado last year; they all help support a child in Africa, and they went to an orphanage to take clothes and gifts to the children there. In doing so, Caitlin and Caleb not only experience a great opportunity to serve others, but their parents are demonstrating and passing on the value of compassion and service.

A normal response, especially for boys, when there is a local or national crisis (or even a tragedy that has touched a family you know) is to want to take some kind of action. In those times, if you brainstorm with your son and together find a constructive way to channel his emotional energy but also express compassion and caring to the victims, the crisis can turn into an opportunity. And doing something to relieve another's suffering, no matter how small, can make an impact and help him heal as well.

Hands-On Values Lessons

Developing your son's values is a lot like building muscles—it takes regular workouts and even daily training. If you are a homeschool mother, you have a myriad of opportunities to develop your children's values every day. If your children go to a school, you can be creative about providing hands-on character lessons.

Let's say you want to build perseverance in your son—you want him to have determination, steadfastness, a stick-to-it nature, and *grit*. I love that word, though it may sound outdated. The movie *True Grit*, which was in theatres not long ago, was a remake of the old John Wayne version. The book and movie featured a fourteen-year-old girl named Mattie Ross, who had tremendous determination. (Note: The original movie is less violent than the 2010 remake, if you want to watch it together.)

But to develop perseverance, it takes more than watching movies. It also takes being engaged in a long-term project—while they are learning some patience and determination along the way. Vegetable gardening is a good hands-on project for this character quality. Growing pumpkins, tomatoes, watermelons, or any vegetable from seeds (preparing the soil, weeding, watering, and all the tasks necessary to grow the plants and wait until the harvest comes) will fill the bill. If you don't have room for a traditional garden, container gardening is also a possibility.

In addition, encourage your son to start a stamp, coin, or rock collection that he develops over time. Adopting an elderly person in a nursing home whom you and your son faithfully visit each week or month, even when you don't feel like it or have a busy schedule, develops perseverance but also a sense of compassion.

My grown daughter, Ali Plum, told me, "Boys' thinking is concrete, so the challenge for me as mother of two sons is taking my own feelings and perceptions and learning to put them in their language, giving concrete reasons why a value or attitude is important." Months ago, she could see her words were falling on deaf ears, and thought, *If they don't listen to me now, what will happen when they are teenagers? If I were a coach and my objective was to win, what would be the essential factors?*

First, Ali identified a couple of values they could pinpoint that would help them win as a family. As she pondered these, it was clearly related to the Golden Rule: living with an attitude of service, gratitude, and kindness. She felt these values would also give her boys success in their relationships and jobs someday. For her, this is not a flowery value system, but essential for life. Internally, she is committed to imparting those values because they offer the biggest opportunities for the world to hear her sons' voices.

She's found that to lecture less and find more real-life examples works best with her boys. Besides posting quotes on the key values around their house in artistic ways, as a family they watched the "30 for 30" sports documentaries on ESPN (see http://30for30.espn.com). Some of the documentaries portray tough situations, but on the whole they contain great lessons for boys, and since Noah and Luke are athletes, they were impacted by the stories of famous sports stars.

Ali and her husband, Hans, say the films prompted good questions from their boys. They would point out things they saw that helped or hurt someone. The parents used that window of time and the time right after each documentary to talk about what they had seen and heard. "And then if I take their cues, I stop talking when they're done!" Ali said. The boys would go back to playing outside, and she walked away knowing those moments had made an impact.

Imparting Values Through Stories

One of our favorite ways to impart values to our children and now our grandchildren is through reading, storytelling, and discussing what we read. When these take place right alongside your positive role modeling, the values you hold dear and want to pass along to your kids are reinforced in an enjoyable way.

Stories give us a sense of who we are and what values our family holds dear, even back a generation or two. When you share about times your grandfather or great-grandfather kept farming in spite of crop failures and obstacles, when you tell a story about how you kept giving your best at a stressful job when you were tempted to throw in the towel, you are passing along strong values.

Children's books in their original form (not Disney or other adaptations) like *The Boy Who Cried Wolf* and *Pinocchio* show the importance of being honest and demonstrate the reality of consequences. Whenever you read aloud classic books like

The Red Badge of Courage by Stephen Crane, *The Hobbit* by
J. R. R. Tolkien, *Charlotte's Web* by E. B. White, *The Black
Stallion* by Walter Farley, or *Treasure Island* by Robert Louis
Stevenson, you are conveying the importance of courage, hard
work, friendship, and patience.

The Chronicles of Narnia by C. S. Lewis were some of our
sons' and daughter's favorites and provided hours of reading
aloud and listening pleasure on family trips. Now they read
these tales to their children. Movies like *Blindside, Hoosiers,*
and *Facing the Giants* portray characters with strong values and
make good discussion starters for boys.

Reading about people who persevered in spite of difficulties
and even failure or tragedy makes a big impact on developing
minds: books about George Washington, Benjamin Franklin
and the founding fathers, great presidents and leaders, World
War II heroes like Eddie Rickenbacker and Louis Zamperini,
and heroes of all wars.

The inspiring true story of Zamperini, a POW in a Japanese
prison camp, is told in a book entitled *Unbroken: A World
War II Story of Survival, Resilience, and Redemption,* and is
well worth reading and relating the story (maybe not the whole
book, as the torture scenes are graphic). Bible characters like
Noah, Joseph, Moses, Daniel, and Joshua, plus modern men
like Chuck Colson and athletes like Dave Dravecky, Tim Tebow,
and Robert G. Griffin III, can make fascinating reads.

Besides books and people in history, keep your eyes open for
current news stories that offer portraits of people of integrity
and strong character. Quotes and wise sayings that relate to the
values you're trying to teach are great to post on the refrigerator
and provide food for thought while your boys are opening the
door for a snack. This is one I posted once by Eleanor Roosevelt:
"All great men have made mistakes. If you're afraid of making a

mistake, then it means you will stop functioning." My daughter posts quotes like "Believe you can and you're halfway there" by Theodore Roosevelt and "One worthwhile task carried to a successful conclusion is worth half-a-hundred half-finished tasks" by Malcolm Forbes.

Family conversation, whether at the dinner table or in the car while you travel or carpool, provides opportunities for sharing values. When you give money to a man on the street holding a sign that says "Please help," and your oldest says, "I think if that man tries finding a job, he wouldn't have to beg," a lively discussion can occur. As a teacher, I've seen that the young people who learn to talk—including agreeing and disagreeing—about moral and ethical issues at home are much better prepared to tackle the difficult decisions they'll face in college and adulthood.

I love what my friend Becky Johnson, who has raised three boys and has grandsons, told me: "Talk about the real men, manly men you know who are good leaders but are very kind to women and children. Talk to your boys about the difference between a tough guy and a real hero." Talk about the men you admire and respect and why you do, such as, "Your granddad Jack was such a gentleman; he treated everyone he met like they were valuable," or "What I love about your uncle is how he is a leader, but he doesn't lead by bossing people around but by serving. What a great man!" By hearing how you appreciate these men, your son gains more understanding of what a good man is and may even desire to be like them someday.

As we continue to shape our sons' values and character, we need to remain teachable. If we're so focused on our boys being a certain way and are attached to what we are teaching them, we may miss an opportunity to see their developing worldview. Let me encourage you to take core lessons or insights, and mixed with their experiences, enjoy the mutual learning that happens.

Little by little, as you get ready for your day, drive your sons to school and sports, have meals together, discuss things, talk and play together, and read bedtime stories, you'll see much character growth that will equip them for fulfillment in school, career, and their own family life.

Questions to Ponder, Journal, or Discuss

1. What are some core values you want your son to internalize and live out in his life? Make a list of the ones that are most important to you.

2. What are the "intangibles" you want to pass on to him, like faith, a sense of adventure, or gratefulness? Which of these are biblical?

3. Think about a few men you most admire and respect. What are the concrete qualities and actions they modeled? Consider sharing these observations with your son.

4. What is one activity or long-term project you could do, perhaps that you read about in this chapter, that would build a core value in your son?

5. What is an area of character your son needs to grow in?

6. Consider the life lessons you have learned, the wisdom that experience has taught. Write it on paper for your son. It can be a good opportunity to sum up your values and share them. What would you start with?

11

A Mom Who Helps Her Son Manage His Emotions

Perhaps the most important thing a mom can do to nurture her son is to be aware of his emotional development.[1]

—Stephen James and David Thomas, *Wild Things*

Some boys get their growth spurt in height by fifth grade; others are the shortest in the class. That is, until ninth grade, when they shoot up like a beanstalk. Some boys talk and read early and others who are just as smart have slower verbal development. Late bloomers in language skills can become avid readers and leaders; late bloomers in athletics can even make it to play on college teams. The important thing is having someone believe in them, to encourage and equip them along the way.

Just as with mental or physical development, boys have differences in their emotional development *and* the rate of growth in knowing how to manage their emotions. While they don't like to have their feelings analyzed and overemphasized by Mom (*How are you feeling? Are you okay—you look sad. . . .*), it helps to gain understanding of boys' emotions.

In our boys' growing-up years, we have the privilege and responsibility of helping them learn to deal with their wide range of feelings: happiness and sadness, enthusiasm and disappointment, guilt, anger, fear, and others.

This is a vital yet daunting role. "Perhaps the most important thing a mom can do to nurture her son is to be aware of his emotional development. Unless she's attentive to this specific area, it's likely that her son's heart will begin to harden," write Stephen James and David Thomas in *Wild Things*.[2]

However, often we aren't certain how to respond to our sons' feelings, especially the negative ones. Studies show that mothers of baby girls interact and comfort them when they show unhappy emotions more than they do with their baby boys. In fact, the mothers tended to ignore their little boys' negative emotions. According to researcher William Pollack, the mothers in the study "were concerned that if they let a boy express too much grief, pain, or vulnerability, somehow he would become something less that a 'real,' fully functioning boy, in accordance with our society's rigid code."[3]

The opposite is true. If a boy is to become a whole person, a really masculine man who can have healthy relationships in adulthood, he needs to be able to acknowledge and manage all his emotions, the negative *and* the positive. He needs to be able to express fear, sadness, anger, and anxiety without being shamed by his parents. While girls tend to talk about their emotions more easily, boys often struggle alone because they aren't comfortable or haven't been coached on how to talk about or deal with their feelings.

That's where you come in, Mom!

"Emotions Charades" and Other Ways to Help Boys Deal With Feelings

I've heard Tiffany, my daughter-in-law, and Ali, my daughter, say to their preteen sons, "What's going on, buddy?" Then, whether they are frustrated with each other, a sibling, or a situation, their moms' question indicates they're willing to hear how their sons are feeling. That's not always easy for boys, however. Even teenagers and adult men are not always in touch with how they are feeling in the moment because of their outward rather than inward focus.

When Caleb was younger, Tiffany and he cut out magazine faces that were sad, happy, afraid, or angry. With some glue and a poster, they made a collage and dialogued about the emotions. "What do you think this person is feeling in this picture?" "How do you know?" or "Have you ever felt this way?"

In elementary school, they played the Emotions Charades game. Each person takes a turn standing up and acting out an emotion like: bored, sad, excited, fearful, or mad. You can write each emotion on a piece of paper and everyone draws one when it's his turn, or they can decide which emotion they want to act out. The other players look at body language, visual clues, and facial expressions of what the different emotions look like on the participants and guess the answer.

Then you can start talking about how each emotion feels: What do you think goes on in your body when you are angry, and then you act that out: hands clenched, stomach churning, eyebrows raised, hands in the air. Then try another one: What does *afraid* look and feel like? How can we tell the difference between the two emotions? The game doesn't have to be long. Not only does it help them get in touch with their own feelings but it helps them recognize those of others as well.

One of the advantages of playing Emotions Charades is that it's not tied to a specific circumstance and not in the middle of a conflict. Your son is probably more relaxed and willing to learn than if there were an actual situation going on. This game is also great for kids who've been through something traumatic and have shut down. It's a safe way for them to get attuned to what emotions look and feel like.

No Cookie-Cutter Boys

One of the great things about the adventure of raising boys is how uniquely each one responds to situations. Every boy has his own emotional style that God has wired within him. No two are exactly alike. The challenge for moms is understanding and responding to those differences.

Michelle Garrett has three boys and one girl. Here's how she describes them and helps them manage their emotions:

The oldest, Jack (now fifteen), can stew with his anger. When he gets grumpy, it's going to last a while. He will close up and refuse to talk sometimes. I don't tolerate that very well, because I am a counselor. And I get curious. Patience and trying to make myself available for when he is ready to talk are what has always worked for us. He is truly a kiddo that needs a little space to think things through and calm down before he can talk. Often what works best is to take him for a drive and a soda, and eventually he will talk.

Brendan, my passionate little man, is the opposite of Jack. He has been nicknamed Benny since he was tiny. If he is angry and gets sent to his room, his anger multiplies. If left alone, he gets completely undone and overwhelmed with his anger. Underneath his anger is a combination of all sorts of hurt and anxiety. Sometimes, I have to set a firm boundary and limits on how he handles his anger. If you don't intervene when Benny is at a feverish pitch, life can pour you out onto the fast lane of a freeway. He can erupt in a volcano of emotion. When his feelings are minimized or judged, he feels alone with this. What he needs is contact and containment. He is an extrovert and what works for him is for me to sit down next to him, listen to him, and help him sort through his situation.

Matthew is a complex little mixture of sweetness, intelligence, and sensitivity. Despite his diagnosis of Asperger's [syndrome], a higher functioning form of autism, he really is pretty easygoing most of the time. When his emotions flare up though, life has to stop for a minute. One of the features of Asperger's and autism is that speech can be slow to develop. This impedes the child's ability to learn how to put words to their own experiences and feelings and then communicate them to others. Another thing that has been slow to develop is his ability to understand social cues and have empathy and connection to others.

What I learned through this experience is that we simply had to take more time to communicate with Matthew. He would often become very anxious and upset when he felt someone was teasing him or didn't understand him. In those moments, we have to say, "Take some deep breaths, and let's figure this out." Then we help him learn how to put words to his experiences and emotions.

While dads encourage their sons to be tough, strong, and brave, mamas offer the safe base of security that allows our sons to venture into this world and take on life's challenges. When our boys are hurt, scared, or feeling a lack of confidence, we can offer them a safe place to come back to and get their feet back under them until they are off on their next adventure.[4]

Calmness in the Midst of the Fray

One key to helping our sons manage their emotions is to be calm and manage *our* emotions. You may be thinking, *How can I be calm when I am so frustrated with my son, or when he's acting out?*

At times little boys can drive us to the end of our rope with their antics. Teenage boys and preteens make thoughtless mistakes and seem to know which of Mom's buttons to push. When their hormones begin to rage, they may become irritable or sensitive, skittish or unpredictable. They need a mom who is relatively calm, patient, and very loving.

One thing a son does not need during adolescence or any other time is a mom in his face, exploding and lacking in self-control. If a mother is too excitable, she may say things she later regrets. The correction or advice she shares are not going to be well received because the conversation is so emotionally charged.

Emotional outbursts are surefire communication busters. If the conversation becomes a shouting match, it's counterproductive. Your son won't be able to process what you say. In the midst of it, he'll tune out, shut down, get out as fast as he can, or explode right back at you. And if you lose your temper frequently, then he will not only lose respect for you but learn by example to behave in a similar way. But there is another way to handle emotions, and that is to understand what's going on in his mind.

My daughter-in-law Tiffany, a family therapist, told me,

> The prefrontal cortex is the learning, problem-solving, and self-control part of the brain. When you're trying to work through conflict and engage in rational thought, that part of the brain doesn't engage while the limbic "fight or flight" system is engaged. When you are upset and adrenalin is flowing, a person wants to fight or take off. When I try to make the teachable moment in the middle of the outburst, no one can learn anything—especially not my son.

If we want our sons to be receptive and hear us, we've got to stay cool and clearheaded. When your hot buttons have been pushed, your body reacts. The signs that you may be on the verge of losing your temper or self-control are a racing heart, feeling hot or flushed, or a louder or higher-pitched voice.

In this case, slow down, take a few deep breaths, and step away from the conversation. One way is to simply say, "I need a time-out," or "Let's talk about this after we've had a chance to cool off." It helps to agree ahead of time on *hand signals* you can each use to signal the need for a break.

If your son is acting out, it will help you to stay calm if you avoid engaging in fearful, catastrophic thinking and projecting twenty years into the future: *With his stubbornness, he's going to turn out just like my brother, the black sheep of the family!* Instead, commit to yourself that you will address the behavior and the consequences, but that correcting it right in the moment may not happen.

If your son continues to become more and more intense and keeps talking, you may have to be a broken record and remind him you won't talk until he is calmer.

"But you promised!" "You're not fair!" "You don't love me!" he may say. It could go on for an hour or more, but eventually he will calm down and there will be a teachable moment and a consequence.

If he goes to his room for a break and settles down, for whatever period of time that is, and you have cooled off, then be sure to come back to the conversation. Listen well and hear your son out. Share your thoughts and your perspective. Come up with a solution or consequence if one is needed, and treat your son with the respect you'd want to be treated with. In doing that, you're being a good role model of handling emotions and communicating well.

If you're a mom who likes to get things settled immediately in a conflict or if you fear in the middle of the outburst, *Oh no, if I don't deal with this bad behavior right now, it will only get worse* . . . it can be challenging to wait! But avoid rushing a boy who processes slower or has trouble verbalizing his feelings. Pushing and hurrying him won't result in resolution but only in more frustration and conflict. It may take him five hours or until the next morning, but he needs time to think about the situation and his part in it.[5]

Helping Boys Deal With Crisis or Loss

In the midst of this journey through childhood and adolescence, a crisis can occur in a boy's family, breaking the rhythm of his growing-up years. The word *crisis* comes from the Greek *krisis*, meaning decision. It connotes a time when we've come to a critical juncture in our lives. It is a turning point, a time when the bottom falls out or everything seems turned upside down. A crisis can be destabilizing, disorienting, and confusing. Without support and understanding, a crisis can overwhelm a young man; he may experience fear and wonder if he or his family can cope.

Children are not exempt from crises and tragedies. Even in the best of neighborhoods and homes young people bear the damaging brunt of a high divorce rate. Violence attacks our youth in both inner-city and suburban schools (instead of "school zone," some school districts have installed "danger zone" signs) and even in a recent tragedy, in movie theatres. In some schools, students have opened fire on innocent classmates. In addition, the Internet has brought all kinds of new destructive activities into the lives of kids.

Young people are profoundly affected by crises in their own lives, in their friends' lives, and in the world around them; yet they respond differently than adults do. They make connections that we would never think about. While the adults in the family may be helped by the community or church, children largely suffer alone—at the time of their greatest need.

When young children hear about a crisis, they may become confused, may regress, experience separation anxiety, and mimic how the adults around them are handling the event. However, their first response is to personalize and even take responsibility for what happened. For example, if houses and neighborhoods in their state are burning, they ask, "Will this happen to me—to our house?" When the next-door neighbors are badly injured in a car accident: "If I am bad, will this happen to my parents too?" When our grandson Caleb (at ten years old) watched the news about the tornadoes that hit several towns surrounding Oklahoma City, he was afraid a tornado was going to destroy their home.

If there is a divorce or death in the family, kids tend to feel guilty, thinking they caused it, or fear it was punishment for their misdeeds. *Why did Dad leave me? Was there something wrong with me, and that's why he didn't stick around?*

Keeping Your Kids Afloat

Cyndi Lamb Curry's husband, Steve, was hit head-on by a drunk teenage driver when Cyndi was six months pregnant with their daughter. She and Steve had two little boys and had been living an active, happy life in Edmond, Oklahoma. But everything changed the Sunday morning of the accident, when Steve was severely brain injured and left in a coma. Doctors were uncertain he would survive. Just seven weeks after the wreck, Cyndi went into the same hospital to deliver their daughter, Kaitlyn, while Steve lay unconscious in a room on another floor.

When he emerged from the coma five months later, he spent another year and a half in the hospital and was left with only

155

mobility in his right arm and hand. He couldn't drive, work, or walk, and had trouble speaking. Five years later, Steve died of leukemia six days after the diagnosis, leaving a grieving widow and three children without a dad.

Cyndi, a courageous and understanding mother to her now grown sons and daughter, shares valuable suggestions for helping kids in her book entitled *Keeping Your Kids Afloat When It Feels Like You're Sinking.*⁶ Since she knows well the heart of a boy, let me share a few of her insights with you:

> Children don't grieve on an even, predictable plane. Grief is a normal response to tragedy, pain, or loss. God designed children with an innate ability to judge how much pain they can handle at one time. They may wait six to nine months to see how the surviving parent is coping before they express their grief.
>
> They may initially respond with sadness but then run outside and play as if nothing happened. They may take their grief down from the shelf (like at bedtime when Dad or Mom used to read to them and they feel her absence acutely), deal with it for a time, cry, talk about the person they miss, and then put their grief away till later.

Some children, particularly boys, express their pain and grief through anger or acting out. They may yell, stomp around, or hit things—or have brief but intense episodes of rage. In these times, it helps to remember that kids need love the most when they are the most unlovable.

One Saturday morning, six months after the accident, Cyndi heard a repetitive thumping outside and went to investigate. Without her son seeing her, she watched as Jeremy picked up rocks and slammed them against the wall. With each blow to the brick wall he yelled, "I hate my life." His whole world had been horribly disrupted, and though he didn't have words to express his pain, with each rock he threw he was acting out the anger and grief.

Cyndi didn't go out and scold Jeremy for throwing the rocks; later that day it opened a small window of opportunity to talk with him about his anguish. While it's not good to berate or shame boys for their feelings (or they will bury them), if they are being destructive, hitting another person, or being overly aggressive, we need to guide them to find non-aggressive ways— like a punching bag in the garage—to release their emotions.

Since younger boys often can't find the words to communicate their feelings, encouraging them to draw or paint a picture can serve as an outlet for expressing their emotions. When they're finished drawing, ask them to tell you their story and listen patiently *if* they are willing to share. If not, give them space and time.

When one of Cyndi's sons, at eleven, found out his father had been diagnosed with leukemia, he told her,

Well, God better not let Dad die. I've prayed for him for years. Every night, at least a million times I've asked God to help Dad walk. God hasn't answered that prayer. And I'm telling you, if He lets my dad die, I'm just not going to believe in Him anymore, and I mean it!

Then he burst into tears. Instead of scolding him or talking or telling him all the good things God had done for them, his mother let him cry and express his deep sorrow for his loss, which helped him to eventually resolve his pain.

Just as we have discussed in this chapter, one of the best lifelines to boys who experience crisis, disappointment, or hurt is to listen to their thoughts and feelings, not to judge them or admonish them to stop feeling like that, and to let them cry when they are sad. Filling their emotional tanks with plenty of love and hugs helps them develop the resiliency to get through troubles and other trials in life.

As you continue connecting with your son and emotionally supporting him, his resiliency, confidence, and ability to be and express who he really is will grow. As William Pollack wrote, "Mothers should feel free to follow what they have always known in their hearts to be the truth—that when he maintains an ongoing connection to his mom, a boy is taking an important, healthy step toward becoming a man."[7]

Questions to Ponder, Journal, or Discuss

1. When you were growing up, how were you taught to deal with your emotions? If you had a brother, was he allowed to express his feelings and emotions, even negative ones?

2. What are your emotional hot buttons? What gets you upset?

3. Are you a "slow burner" (it takes a lot for you to get angry or upset, but when you do, you carry it around and do a "slow burn")? Or are you a person with intense emotions who explodes and then everything feels fine to you?

4. What is your son's emotional style and his triggers for anger or depression?

5. Has your son or family experienced a tragedy or crisis? How did your son express his emotions?

12

A Mom Who Nurtures
Her Son's Faith

It is faith rather than formula, grace rather than
guarantees, steadfastness rather than success that
bridges the gap between our own parenting efforts,
and what, by God's grace, our children grow up to
become.[1]

—Leslie Leyland Fields

One Sunday morning the first winter we lived in Maine, it was
nine degrees below zero and had snowed all night. The roads
hadn't been cleared yet, so we were snowbound and unable to
drive to the little church we attended in town. So I thought it
would be nice to have church at home and a little spiritual time
together. Holmes led us in prayer and read a Psalm aloud. Then
it was time for my creative activity. I gave a sheet of white paper
to each person in the family and said, "We're going to draw
a picture that shows how we're doing with God and how we

feel about Him. Let's all do that." I thought surely this would stimulate some good discussion.

It was quiet for a while as each one thought and sketched. Then we shared. Alison's picture was a big heart with a little girl inside it. "That's me, close to God's heart," our eleven-year-old said. Chris, thirteen, showed us his very detailed picture of a brick window ledge and a boy dressed just like him in khaki pants and polo shirt (that he got teased for at Yarmouth Junior High) barely hanging on to the windowsill. "That's how I feel right now. In a new school and unfamiliar place, I'm hanging on to God."

When it was our fifteen-year-old son's turn, he held up a blank sheet of paper and said nothing. A few seconds later, he turned and walked upstairs to his room. As I heard the door close and looked at that blank piece of paper, my heart sank.

Laying the Foundation

Like you, I purposed to build a foundation of faith in our kids' lives. I believe each of us who are believing parents are called to teach our children God's ways and gently lead them to Jesus Christ, in response to Luke 18:16 (NLT): "Let the children come to me. Don't stop them! For the Kingdom of God belongs to those who are like these children" and "Anyone who welcomes a little child like this on my behalf is welcoming me" (Matthew 18:5 NLT). I'm always moved by these verses because I love children, not only my own. But also for the great love expressed in these passages that reveal the heart God has for all of His children, but especially the young ones and His desire to have relationship with them.

While it's never too early or too late, the first six years are a golden opportunity to nurture your son's faith. In these years, they spend time thinking and wondering about God: *Who made me? Who made people? What purpose are we here for?* During the season that home and family are the center of his world, you have a chance to sow lots of seeds and for them to learn about God's love as you point out His blessings in a spring rain, a brilliant firefly, or a spectacular sunset. Whenever you read Bible stories to your son, you're giving him snapshots of God and the way He works in people's lives.

You're nurturing your son's faith when you talk about God as you go along in your day, in the Deuteronomy 6 way of developing spiritual foundations—to naturally talk about His Word "when you are at home and when you are on the road, when you are going to bed and when you are getting up" (vv. 6–7 NLT).

You're also laying the foundation for your son's attitude about God by the loving relationship you develop with him. Kids see God through the filter of Mom and Dad (no pressure!). We are the first picture of their heavenly Father. Our love reflects His love, a love so wide and deep that He gave His only Son for their salvation. Our acceptance reflects His acceptance, our being there and being faithful to our marriage and family reflects in a small way God's forever faithfulness to His children.

Kids are impacted by the small things that make up our interaction. Caleb, my grandson, told me this about his mom: "The best thing is how my mom is understanding and kind to me. How comforting she is when something bad has happened. If something's really hard in my life or I'm worried about my grades or a project, she prays for me. She asks others to pray for me too. When there's a tennis tournament or a big basketball game I'm nervous about, she encourages me to do it instead of backing down and taking the easy way out. My mom loves me all the time. She's always there for me." This is a boy who doesn't have a hard time believing that there is a loving God.

Stages of Faith Development

In the many years I taught children's Sunday school and church, I found Art Murphy's perspective on faith development very helpful.[2] Murphy is founder and president of Arrow Ministries (www.arrowministries.com) and the author of *The Faith of a Child* (Moody Publishers). Understanding kids' spiritual development is valuable when you want to encourage their faith. During his more than thirty years as a minister to children and families (including thousands of personal interviews with children and parents), Murphy detected four distinct stages of spiritual development in children.

Children begin with the **Discovery Stage,** which lasts from birth to age seven. During these years, they soak up all they see and experience through the way parents, siblings, teachers, and friends act. Also through hearing Bible stories and television programs, soaking in verses learned in Sunday school and school activities. These are years of pretending and magical thinking as they wonder: *Is God like Santa Claus or the tooth fairy? Is God powerful like the Force but also someone who watches over us and gives away toys and pets?* Curiosity is at a high point during this stage, and kids ask many questions as they watch, think, and discover the world around them.

The **Discerning Stage** comes next, beginning with the early elementary grades. Questions become more specific and direct: *Is heaven real or not? What is it like? Are we going there? What happened to Grandpa when he died? How about our dog? How do you get to be a Christian? I want to ask Jesus into my stomach.* (This last real comment by an eight-year-old reflects the misinformation that often gets mixed into their thoughts.)

It's easy to think these questions mean our son is ready to make a serious commitment to Christ, but Murphy tells parents, "Life is coming, but it may not be delivery time." What's *most important* during these years is to model a joyful faith as we assist our sons in learning about Jesus through the Bible and through prayer . . . and to be alert to the Lord's timing.

"We're the pediatricians, but God is the obstetrician; He has their spiritual birth date planned just like He did their physical birthday," Murphy told me. So we don't have to worry. Some kids understand what it means to follow Christ; "I love Jesus with all my heart" can't be ignored. Others aren't ready yet. Instead of pushing, even if all the other children in his church group have made a commitment, we can listen, ask questions, and pray with and for our son. And as we do, we'll understand his heart and unique spiritual development a little better.

In the **Deciding Stage,** your son may begin to sense his own need for God. He may open his heart or feel convinced he wants to make Christ his Lord. Our son Chris was nine when he told us one day that he decided he wanted to be baptized. "I want to follow Jesus. I've already asked Him to be my Lord."

We weren't sure if it was the Bible verses that had been planted in his mind and heart since he was a little boy, the fact that his grandma had died the year before and he'd thought about heaven, our prayers, or if he just felt a need for God. In any case, it was God's right time for our son; his commitment was real, and much to our joy, a few weeks later he was baptized. It helps at all stages for the parents' faith to be real and personal, for God to be spoken of in the home, and Christianity to be much more than a program or production we take our kids to at church.

In the **Discipleship Stage,** it's a season for growth, starting with what I call "taking our children praying" (which I prefer rather than "teach them to pray"). This is the time to encourage and model natural, conversational prayer that isn't just for Sundays or bedtime. Talk to God as you and your son walk together around the block or drive in the car, knowing the Lord is always listening and acts on behalf of those who call on Him.

The Discipleship Stage is a good time to help get your son grounded in the Bible and growing in his relationship with Jesus. By reading and discussing the Bible together, applying it to whatever your son is facing each day, you help his roots grow deeper in Christ.

Anne Graham Lotz says, "In the race of life, the 'baton' is the truth that leads to personal faith in God. Each generation receives the 'baton' from the previous generation, runs the race to the best of its ability, then passes the 'baton' smoothly and securely to the next generation."[3]

Being a part of a Christian fellowship is important so your son can connect and grow in friendship with other people in God's family, children and grown-ups alike. It means a lot when a boy knows that he isn't alone in the spiritual journey through life but has a support system. Serving others is an important part of discipleship—and a key to keeping kids engaged in a faith journey—so that they get to experience the joy of being used by God to bless someone else.

The discipleship process is a lengthy one, which takes years and continues throughout our lives. Isn't it marvelous how patient God is with us, His children, in our spiritual starts and stops, in two steps forward and three steps backward and the zigzag journey many of us take as He conforms us to the image and nature of Christ. Lord, grant that we will be as patient with our children as you are with us!

Through each of these faith stages, we don't need to manipulate, push, or pull, but instead come alongside. We can share our own current spiritual experiences and how God has worked in our lives without being preachy.

As we respect the inner time clock and how faith develops and matures in each of our children, we learn to trust God's timetable for them. While we encourage them to connect with God in their daily lives, we need to let go of our expectations of what that's going to look like.

Russ Page of San Antonio, Texas, is grateful for how his mother led him and gave him room to grow:

> The ways you nurtured my faith . . . prayed for me and my siblings and modeled prayer, took us to church, allowed me to see (eventually) the gift of revealed sin and the loving consequences. You served our family by making meals, cleaning clothes, and always driving me and my friends around. You never said *no* when I asked you to buy me a Christian music CD. I'm not sure how much was taught versus caught but there was a lot to catch, so thank you, Mom!

Are there any guarantees that if we do our part of spiritual nurturing, we will be rewarded by sons who automatically follow God? Even when we do our best, it may not work that way—that is, on our time schedule. As Leslie Leyland Fields said,

> We must be clear about our own limits. We are not capable of producing perfect followers of Christ, as if we were perfect ourselves. Our work cannot purchase anyone else's salvation or sanctification. . . . We will parent imperfectly, our children will make their own choices, and God will mysteriously and wondrously use it all to advance his kingdom.[4]

Some of the most stellar, devoted Christian parents I have known have had quite a different outcome with their children's spiritual walk than they'd imagined: Our dear friends, who are extremely committed believers and former missionaries, and who devoted themselves to raising their children, had a son in prison last year. Another mom who came to a prayer group I attended had a son struggling with drug addiction.

There are many adult children who are good people but not connecting in a deep way with God: One dear young man we've known since his childhood is a seeker, following an Eastern religion despite being brought up in a loving Christian home, and another has merely walked away from the faith.

In the thousands of young people and parents he's met in more than thirty-five years of ministry, Joe White, founder and president of Kanakuk Kamps, observed: "Great parents can have prodigal children. Horrible parents can have great children. Some parents have kids on both ends of the spectrum—same environment, different outcomes."[5]

We would love to bring all our sons and daughters to God's throne of grace and see them in adulthood choose the faith we chose for them. Like many mothers, I've said, "I have no greater joy than to hear that my children are walking in the truth" (3 John 1:4) and prayed that they would. Oh, how we desire for our sons to be fully committed to God. Yet while we are assigned the responsibility of laying the foundations of faith, we can't make any person follow Christ—even, and especially not, our offspring. We can't will or manage their spiritual "success."

What God asks of us isn't a badge of honor because our kids are spiritual winners, but for us as mothers and fathers to be faithful, to love Him with all our hearts and trust the rest of the process to Him. After all, as Leslie Leyland Fields has said,

> We are not sovereign over our children—only God is. Children are not tomatoes to stake out or mules to train, nor are they numbers to plug into an equation. They are full human beings wondrously and fearfully made. Parenting, like all tasks under the sun, is intended as an endeavor of love, risk, perseverance, and above all, faith.[6]

Will You Keep Following Me?

When Jake was born, Lindy asked God for a Scripture that would guide her prayers for her son and reflect His will for him, and Matthew 28:19, "Therefore go and make disciples of all nations . . ." seemed clearly to be the life verse God gave her. She thought, *If Jake's going to be a disciple maker, he needs to be a disciple. So how do I shape this little disciple for you, Lord?*

She and her husband did everything possible to nurture Jake's faith—praying for him before he was born, sharing Bible stories when he was young, reading through the whole Bible every year as a family. They were a verbal family and talked about God and everything else in their home. They prayed together and took Jake to church and Sunday school. He went to great Christian camps every summer through his senior year.

Yet many years after she received the verse in Matthew for her son, Lindy is still waiting. In between there have been some difficult years. Jake's adolescence was stormy, to say the least. It was as if overnight, he went from "Mommy, I love you to the moon and back" to "I hate you."

He struggled in school, was teased, but didn't always let his parents know. He tried to do the work, but found it really hard and he had trouble focusing. They had no alcohol in their home, but Jake started drinking at age thirteen, and a neighborhood friend exposed him to pornography around the same time. A change of schools didn't help. Counseling helped a little, but this mom grew desperate to change things and fix the situation.

They got stricter with their son, which didn't help. The counselor suggested taking the door off his bedroom, which didn't help. Many times they overreacted instead of responding—which didn't help at all. Jake would talk and his mom would advise and lecture. Their conversations turned into arguments.

167

He didn't want to have anything to do with church—or his parents.

Finally God seemed to say to Lindy, *If your son hates you and doesn't follow me until you die, will you still trust me?* This was a big question, because she had thought the *one thing* that would kill her heart was if her kids didn't follow the Lord. She wanted that above all else and felt she'd be a failure if they didn't. *Will you keep loving me and following me if he never comes back to me or to you?* God questioned. *And would you put your hands behind your back and let me work?*

Through tears, Lindy released Jake and committed to loving and following God regardless of what happened with her son. In the years after this encounter, they stayed connected with their son, who lives in another state. The relationship between Jake and his parents has been in recovery and healing mode. "I think I was too often angling for opportunities to bring Christ into our conversations," she told me. "When I gave my heart's desire to God, it was just natural to love my son freely, without reserve, and let the Holy Spirit do His job of developing the relationship between God and my son." She's learned to listen better and really hear what Jake is saying, give him respect and admiration for the good things he's doing in his career and how he's helping young people. Because of his own struggles in adolescence, he understands and knows how to reach out and communicate with the kids he works with. And he loves his parents more than ever.

Has he turned around in his spiritual life or grown closer to God?

Years and years later, this mom is still waiting. But she waits with hope and trust now, watching God weave His purpose and patterns into Jake's and her story. She knows God has His plan for Jake and His way of doing things.

Getting Creative

Sometimes we moms need to be creative in planting seeds of God's Word in our sons' lives. When Elaine, my dear friend since Baylor days, and her husband had their last son at home after raising four older boys, they had made a big move from the Dallas area to the country near the tiny town of Celeste. Matthew had given up Christian school and all things Christian and now had to go to a public school, the only one in the area. He was very unhappy for over a year.

His mother realized that the end of the day was challenging and often her husband was traveling. So she read Matthew biographies of a Christian boy or man whose life demonstrated that *God sees you through.*

Then she decided what he needed was for God's Word to be the last thing he heard before leaving the house for his public middle school. "My words as a mom were not the impact of God's truth," Elaine told me.

"So every morning as he was eating breakfast, I read Matthew the *Daily Light.*[7] All of our boys knew the importance of this little treasure. My grandfather, a missionary doctor in China, was captured by the Japanese during World War II and imprisoned. But his partner doctor was able to sneak him his copy of *Daily Light* before he was hauled away to prison camp.

"I know today that God's Word will not return to Him void, that the repetition of those verses each morning through middle, junior high, and high school helped implant truth in Matthew and provide a barrier against the world's assault," Elaine shared.

She later realized Matthew had found some tapes she'd gotten from a missionary, brief recordings of sixty stories of life among the Belgian Congo people. In the quiet of his room, he listened to those stories every night on a tape player throughout junior high and high school. Hearing of God's love, protection, and work influenced him greatly.

Adolescents and Faith

Part of growing up and becoming an adult is "sorting through your beliefs and experiences to choose how to integrate them and live them out," says Dr. Catherine Hart Weber, psychologist and coauthor of *Is Your Teen Stressed or Depressed?* Who questions and who doesn't, she says, is more related to personality and temperament than being a rebellious or a "good" person. Some teens are very private about their faith and others are verbal about it, telling you exactly how they feel.

Says Dr. Weber,

> Strong, independent personalities test and question everything, including spiritual issues. They don't want to just read somebody else's view in a book or follow what their parents say. Compliant, submissive kids tend to follow what they were taught growing up . . . at least for a while.
>
> Yet those young people who follow along with a "coattail" faith may never question until midlife when a crisis pushes them into finding their own spiritual foundations. What's occurring may be just a delayed phase of individuating spiritually.[8]

Questioning and doubting are part of seeking, an entirely normal part of the process of separating from parents and standing on their own two feet—spiritually as well as in other ways. Young people and adult sons want their own spiritual journey to be respected, not put down or devalued.

Yet it can be anxiety producing when you hear that a high percentage of young people forsake their faith when they leave high school and don't come back in the adult years. Anxiety can throw us into overdrive, trying to get our teenagers to go to church or Bible study.

"Parents often find themselves trying to teach or even just encourage their adolescents' Christian walk only to find their 'little flock' rolling their eyes or secretly trying to send a text message," said Dr. Ken Wilgus. In fact, in the hundreds of children, teens, and parents he's counseled over the years, he observes that the number-one reason young men leave the faith is a power struggle with their parents.

What are some ways we can influence our teenager's faith without a power struggle, so that their individuating/separating from us doesn't get mixed with rebellion against God? One is to realize some of the pitfalls. According to Ken, the top three turnoffs for teens or preteen boys are:

- Not practicing what we preach, all the while being preachy and lecturing
- Fear-based Christianity
- Controlling and trying to regulate their relationship with God

Ken advises parents to look for ways to slowly release control, even on required church attendance. At fourteen, you might say, "You don't have to go to this youth event. But we do want you to go to church with us." Look for ways you can be flexible. If your fifteen-year-old wants to go to youth group with his friend at another church, you could allow that and be grateful he desires to go.

In addition, boys need to see faith in the men around them. Hopefully your son's father will model a genuine faith. But also look for opportunities for him to be surrounded by other faithful men or to have a trusted mentor, who is involved or close to the family, especially if you are a single mom.

Ken also suggests that parents acknowledge to their adolescents *sometime before they leave home* (and not just the last

semester of their senior year) that they are young adults in the
faith. Let them know they are about to launch out on their
own, making their own decisions and choosing to follow or not
follow God. Talk to them about the fact that you can't make
them believe or follow a certain way. In addition, Ken advises,

> Prayerfully plan for the right age to let your adolescent choose
> for themselves about participation in church—and let them know
> that day will come. A parent's respect for the sanctity of their
> child's own response to Christ's call may be the surest guide we
> can offer once they have grown past their need to follow our lead.[9]

If your son is in the "far country," living with a heart that
is away from his Creator, let me encourage you to never give
up praying for your son. Keep believing that the Lord is able to
accomplish His purposes and weave His plan for good into his
life. As John Henry Jowett says,

> God's ability to perform is far beyond our prayers—even our
> greatest prayers! . . . I have asked for a cupful, while He owns
> the entire ocean! I have asked for one simple ray of light, while
> He holds the sun! My best asking falls immeasurably short of
> my Father's ability to give, which is far beyond that which we
> could ever ask.[10]

Questions to Ponder, Journal, or Discuss

1. Dialogue with your child or teen about one or more of
   the following questions:

   - How are you and God doing? Can you draw a picture
     of how you feel about the relationship?

   - What do you think about our devotional times as a
     family? Our church?

- What do you wish we would do to better connect with God and each other?

What did *you* learn from your son's responses?

2. Where is your son along the path of spiritual journey: the Discovery, Discerning, Deciding, or Discipleship Stage, or somewhere in between?

3. If you have a teenager or young adult son, what helps him engage with spiritual issues? What helps him engage with God?

4. Does your son have faithful men he can observe or be connected to who love and serve God? If not, where could you find this resource?

5. There isn't a one-size-fits-all journey to Christ for everyone. God is creative in his pursuit of His children. How did you come to faith? Thinking about your own journey can help you have more patience and hope for your son.

13

A Mom Who Releases Her Son to Manhood

When it is time for him to take that final step out of boyhood into the country of men, may you have the courage to let him go, so that he can live as fully as he was created to be, with confidence, character, and compassion.[1]

—Stephen James and David Thomas, *Wild Things*

As I was looking in the mirror, putting on makeup the morning after Justin and Tiffany's wedding, I thought I heard Justin's voice echo from upstairs through the house. He had lived with us for a few weeks after college graduation, so I'd heard his wonderful, distinct voice in the house as I had during his eighteen years of growing up. Reflections of those years, the college years, as well as the wedding festivities swept through my memory in those moments. But suddenly it hit me.

Justin doesn't live here anymore.

The weekend had been memorable. All our family and friends had gathered at the church on the sunny May afternoon, as our son and his beautiful bride became Mr. and Mrs. Justin Oliver Fuller—the first of our children to be married.

A tear slipped from my eye and down my cheek. Justin and Tiffany had left for their honeymoon in Colorado. But when they returned, they would live in their own apartment in Norman, Oklahoma, while Tiff finished her senior year of college.

It wasn't the first time Justin had left home. Between his four years of college, he'd come home for holidays and to live with us most summers while he worked. But this time, our son wasn't coming back. As bittersweet as this reality was, it was what we'd been preparing him for all along . . . to leave us and begin his own life.

Stephen James and David Thomas write, "A powerful paradox of motherhood is that if you do your job well, your son will leave you completely."[2] And sure enough, Justin had.

I'd let go and entrusted our son to God in prayer hundreds of times over the years—when he was in the ER, when he went to a new school, when he went to his first weeklong camp, when he left for college nine hours away. All of that was good preparation. But this was the final releasing . . . into his role as husband, into his future, and into his role as leader of his own family. Mission accomplished!

When God Calls

A son needs a mom who knows when God calls her to release him to manhood. The first time my prayer partner Peggy Stewart sensed her oldest son was separating from her was during John's senior year of high school. He had been the most communicative of her four sons. When they talked, John listened to his mom and was responsive about what she advised.

Yet suddenly it seemed they were at odds. He was becoming edgy, sharing less, and pulling away. Even though it's an important part of a son's masculine journey, it felt strange. She didn't know it, but, "In order to move fully into the world of masculinity, he must leave the world of femininity."[3]

God showed Peggy that her son was the budding head of a new household. The season of God's nurturing John through her was coming to an end and a new season was beginning for him. It was no longer fitting for her to dominate this young man whom God was calling to be the eventual head of a new household. When she did try to dominate and manage him, they had conflict.

There is a profound parallel in this emergence of our sons into manhood. At birth, the Lord brought this new person into the world through his mother. That process wasn't pretty, painless, or predictable. In a similar way, the "birthing" of our son out of the nurturing care of his mother and into the passageway of adulthood often isn't pretty, painless, or predictable either. And the maturation date is different for each son, depending on how he's moving through his developmental journey.

In *Ragman and Other Cries of Faith,* Walter Wangerin says the pain of childbearing is not a single event:

> It's twofold and it comes twice; and I am astonished by the love revealed in such a miracle. First . . . a woman must make space in her body for a baby. . . . [Then] she must empty the space. It does not matter how much she has invested in carrying the child. At the end of nine months she's asked to give [him] up . . . to deliver him whole and squalling into existence.[4]

But this labor isn't enough! As mothers we are asked to do it all over again! We sacrifice many things to give our child space to grow: our schedule, our time, our sleep, our beauty, and perhaps our career. But at the same time we experience much joy as we see our child begin to walk, talk, build, learn, and grow.

But then at the child's maturity, we experience the "second suffering," when we must "birth our child" out of our house and into the world as an independent being. As Wangerin explains:

> It does not matter how much she has invested in raising him. By stages, now, she labors to let him go. By degrees she loosens the reins, knowing full well the dangers to which she sends her child, yet fearing the greater danger of clinging to him forever. And now her hurt is the hurt that *he* will encounter on his own. (Will he survive in a careless existence, and thrive?) And beside that, her hurt is loneliness. To be, he must first be *gone*.
> This is childbearing at its most laborious.[5]

Leaving the Nest

If you're a mother of young boys, or middle-schoolers, I'm glad you're reading this chapter. Because actually the process of our children leaving the nest starts way before you take them to their college campus or they're headed out for the honeymoon with their precious bride. And it's important to get a big-picture perspective of what the end goal of all our parenting is.

The first day your son picks up his new superheroes (or Avengers or Iron Man) lunch bag, walks to the big yellow school bus, and rides out of your sight, the releasing process has begun. At that point, you may run right into the need to entrust him to God . . . until you pick him up that afternoon.

Letting go of our sons is a natural, universal process that happens in stages and in defining moments—but sometimes it doesn't feel so natural. Whatever we call it—releasing, letting go, relinquishing—when we sense God nudging us to let go of our dear one or the circumstances demand it, it can be challenging to our mother's heart. After all, moms were made for nurturing their kids, not giving them up and letting them go!

According to researchers Stephen James and David Thomas,

> To some degree, every mother has a natural instinct to protect her children. The trick for moms of boys is to foster a balance between his desire for adventure, exploration, and separation and her desire for a healthy, nurturing, and safe environment— without erecting barriers to her son's ability to assert himself as an individual.[6]

Balancing nurture and separation—easier said than done. Mothers of teens often fear that something bad will happen to their sons or that they'll make a bad choice if they release them to God. It can be a scary proposition to see your sixteen-year-old drive off in the family car with only a friend in the front seat or head across the world for a mission trip to Africa.

When her twin sons moved several hundred miles away, a mother confided to me, "All these years I've spent caring for, loving, feeding, and protecting my sons, and now they're such great guys I enjoy so much and *they're leaving me*? And God's asking me to let go? It's almost too much to ask!"

When our son is gone, the house seems quieter and emptier without his energy and noise. We may even miss his messy room, loud music, and all those mounds of stinky socks and gym clothes we washed over the years.

Holding On: A Pitfall of the Process

"I needed my mom to release me to be my own person," a man in his thirties told me. "Because my parents got a divorce when I was eleven years old, it was expected that I would be the man of the house. I felt like I had no teen years; I lost adolescence because my mom needed me to be a grown-up."

This young man had a need to be independent but got a lot of resistance from his mother. He wanted to be released from feeling like he had to care for her (though she wasn't ill), fix her, or solve her problems. He wanted to have friends and start developing his own life, not be responsible for things that adults are supposed to do.

Finally, with God's grace, he moved far away for college and graduate school to separate from his mother and become his own man, eventually marry and have a child. His mother loved him dearly, he knows, but added, "Our relationship would be much better today if I hadn't been expected to carry the burden I did."

You can avoid this trap by not making your son the "man around the house" or telling him he needs to take care of you even if you are a single mother. God is well able to be your Husband and the Father of your son.

When mothers depend on their sons (or daughters, for that matter) too much, either to be the man who's absent or for their primary friend or confidant, it creates a tension and unhealthy ties that are hard for sons to break. He's not the rescuer, the one you lean on, or a knight in shining armor. It's not his job to be counselor or therapist—and intimate details and emotional or marriage problems are too big a burden for him to bear.

Cultivate your own friendships, and once your son has left home, begin to think of him as an adult friend among your other friends. When he shows that he has a need for space, respect it and know that at a different point, you'll come back together. Then as he leaves home, your son will be freer to live his life and develop his own identity, friendships, and interests—and have more desire at some point to connect with you.

In addition, try not to keep helicopter parenting (you could use the word *hovering* if you prefer it) when your son is in college. One college professor, Kathleen Volk Miller, described students at the university where she teaches like this: "What I see is self-reliance being thwarted at every turn. I know a mother who watches the surveillance cams at her son's school for hours, hoping he will randomly walk by the camera. Another requests her college kids' syllabuses, puts exam and project dates in her own calendar and sends them reminders."[7]

The majority of college students get daily calls from their parents, but Mom and Dad don't know all the creative ways their kids hide from them. Many have fake Facebook pages they use only for parents; they save the real Facebook page for their friends. They get frustrated when Mom "friends" their pages and then does surveillance on their activities and relationships through Facebook and Twitter. Their cell phones become a crutch and foster dependence when they text dear Mom asking for cash on a regular basis and then go online to transfer the funds, as one male student did right before he walked in a bar where he spent a chunk of the deposit.

Professor Miller suggests and practices with her own college kids the following: Give them some space, being less like the pilot and more like the ramp agent (who gives direction to help the plane fly into its gate but doesn't try to take over the controls and fly the plane, waves the flags on the tarmac if the plane isn't coming in to the right gate, unloads and reloads the bags and other tasks to get the plane turned around and ready for its next flight). Avoid hovering around his life via phone or Internet and swooping in to solve your college-aged children's problems. Instead, back off a bit and trust as they navigate the bumpy freedoms of being a young adult.[8]

Preparing the Way

While there can be lots of tears when we leave our beloved son on the campus in another state and drive away, not every mother feels sad when her son leaves home. Because we are individuals, there are different ways mothers cope with this departure. Some feel a great sense of fulfillment and joy that they have worked themselves out of a job.

That's how Melinda felt. She enjoyed her two sons and daughter while they were at home. Yet she was pragmatic about the transition to adulthood. "I wasn't really sad, because leaving home is part of growing up. I always saw it as the next phase. I love my kids, but I did not want to take care of them for their whole lives!" she told me.

Throughout their childhood and adolescence, Melinda had held the long perspective that it's the parents' job to grow their kids and teach them to live independently so they'll be *prepared to leave*. As a result, when they made choices, her sons had to accept the consequences with no rescuing from Mom. If they had a school assignment and went out with friends and didn't do it, she didn't save them or do it herself so they wouldn't fail. She allowed them to learn from the natural consequences. She supported them but didn't fix things to make it easier. And she didn't protect them from reality.

Each family member helped with housework. The boys weren't given allowances but what was needed was provided. Any money they had was a birthday gift or earned from work. John delivered papers and the other son worked at a local fast-food restaurant in the summers.

The preparation process continued in the junior high years, when Mom gave them their own clothing money and they got to manage it. If they wanted to buy name-brand jeans or other high-ticket items, they had to earn more money. Lo and behold,

Target and Walmart clothes started looking better to the boys. As a result of that and other preparation, Melinda's kids were ready to leave for college. She and her husband helped with their education so they would graduate from college debt-free and bought them a used car upon graduation.

"When it was time for each of them to launch, I was like 'Hooray—we did it!'" she said.

In contrast, some mothers feel a void or become depressed when their sons leave the nest for college—especially if they have enjoyed going to all their football games or cheering them on at sports events, band, and choir performances. Moms often miss being needed and involved in their sons' lives. One mom told me she felt a bit thrown aside and doomed to loneliness except for a rare visit at holidays and an occasional phone call. If your son is the last child to take off, life can feel a little empty and you can feel dispensable. The page has turned and that chapter of active parenting is over.

Well, keep in mind, Mom—*he'll be back*! Maybe your son will return at holidays or summer break. If so, that period of time will have its own challenges—especially if you try to enforce a curfew when he's been living on his own for a semester or a year. And someday your son and your daughter-in-law may walk in the door with a baby in tow, and your house will again be filled with the laughter, mess, and fun that children bring.

The Upside to Kids Leaving Home

While becoming an empty nester can trigger intense emotions in moms, I also know some big, strong dads who wept when their sons left home for college. Yet there is an upside to our children leaving, and it helps to think about the benefits, because there are a number of them!

When the full-time parenting role is over, marital happiness tends to increase. As our grown children get older and are doing well, we feel joy about how they are handling life (without us!) and achieving their goals. You might experience gratefulness that your son is a responsible, capable person. When our kids leave home, we have more freedom to pursue things we really enjoy but had put on the back burner because of a lack of time.

You can reconnect with friends, plan a trip, take an art class if you've always wanted to paint, start a business, learn to tap dance or sculpt. When they leave, your connection with your grown children isn't over; you may even cultivate a better relationship and enjoy each other more as adult friends.

The Launching Pad

Since releasing our sons to manhood is inevitable and some of the most important work of motherhood, let's get prepared instead of dreading it. Spiritually, we need to get our faith in gear. As San Diego pastor Miles McPherson says,

> When you entrust your child to God, your faith often has to go back to basics: believing that God exists, that He is the giver of all good gifts to all those who believe, that He indeed cares for you and your family as much as the Bible says He does.[9]

Then let's see how we can prepare them step-by-step for that eventual transition to manhood:

Encourage steps toward autonomy. Rather than resisting your adolescent son's God-given desire to be independent, foster it. Little by little, transfer responsibilities and control to him so that when he leaves, he won't need you. Allow him to make his own decisions about certain areas. (For some good ideas, reread chapter 3 on building confidence.)

Communicate that you're supporting his growing up and out. At a certain age, maybe fourteen or fifteen, sit down and talk with your son. In your own words say, "In just a few short years, you're going to be on your own. You won't be under our roof or authority—you'll be leaving to launch out on your own life. We want to prepare you for that." That diffuses a lot of conflict between you and your no-longer-a-child and growing-into-manhood son—because ultimately, the more we try to control them, the more they will resent and resist us.

When your son takes a little leap or a bound toward independence, avoid perceiving that as rejection; it just brings guilt and manipulation into the relationship. The more we take their attempts to separate and be autonomous personally, the more frustrated we'll both be—because the truth is, it's not all about us. It's all about our son coming to a new place in his development and *growing up*! And that is ultimately a God-designed process and a marvelous thing. Dr. Ken Wilgus explains this well:

> The primary source of strain between adolescents and their parents today is because the heart of a teenager starts tracking for signs of "growing up."
>
> The primary need of adolescents is called "individuation," which means that adolescents need more than anything to know "when will I be an adult and how will I get ready for it?" Since our culture provides no set means of celebrating this transition, families are left to slug it out on their own. The result is often a tension between teenagers pressing for autonomy and parents trying to provide protection and counsel to their increasingly resentful kids.[10]

I admire the way Lynda Hunter Bjorklund celebrated her son Clint's transition by planning something very special for him. He'd grown up without his dad, so she began thirty-one days before his thirteenth birthday, and together they read one proverb each night with him. She gave him intermittent "boy gifts" through that month (flashlight, alarm clock, thank-you notes, and stamps), and taught him one stanza from Rudyard Kipling's poem "If":

> If you can talk with crowds and keep your virtue,
> Or walk with Kings—nor lose the common touch,
> If neither foes nor loving friends can hurt you,
> If all men count with you, but none too much:
> If you can fill the unforgiving minute
> With sixty seconds' worth of distance run,
> Yours is the Earth and everything that's in it,
> And—which is more—you'll be a Man, my son![11]

On Clint's actual birthday, she invited several men who had been involved in his life in some way. She asked them to come to a lasagna dinner and bring an old or new tool and a letter passing on a life lesson.

> His pastor came with a tool belt and talked about the importance of always telling the truth (Ephesians 6:14). An air force football player brought a level and talked about the importance of balance. His principal and coach gave him a compass and talked about seeking godly guidance (Psalm 37:23).[12]

In this creative way, she celebrated her son's journey from childhood to his adolescent years.

Avoid over-mothering, which can get in the way of adolescent boys' developing independence and coming to know the vision that God has for them and their lives. Michelle Garrett told me:

> My boys don't need to discover those things in their lives as long as I continue to shelter and overprotect them and be their God. Another message I send to them by over-mothering is that they are not strong enough to deal with their own failures, their own

emotions, and their own consequences. In doing this, we can compromise their developing resiliency, courage, and a creative God-vision for their future. And we take away their need for God.[13]

If you have a son with special challenges or needs, it can be much more difficult to let go. Sometimes our son will get bumped or hurt. Sometimes he will fail or make a mistake.

Jan told me,

> Even before our son got sick at age six, we were the helicopter parents, controlling and micromanaging. My motto was "anticipate and prevent." I would tell him what to do and not to do, and try to mold him into what is socially acceptable. I began to realize when I was hovering over him, wanting it to go so well that I had crushed his spirit.

As a result of the strep-induced neurological disorder, her son Jared had a hard time in social situations. He loves kids and interacting with them, but they often didn't like to be with him. Their daughter was the social butterfly, invited to friends' houses all the time, but her brother was left at home isolated, without friends except for his parents. His mom's heart ached for him.

When Jared was twelve, a turning point occurred. He was going to the school dance, and his mother had gone shopping to pick out a nice button-up shirt like the other boys would be wearing.

"Just a few pointers and then I'll let him go." As she tucked the shirt in his new jeans and was just about to lovingly pummel him with advice, she had to step back and battle within. God reminded her, "Even though you are afraid a train wreck is coming in a situation, don't try to mold him into what's socially acceptable. Let him be the creative and quirky kid that he is."

Although she wanted to advise, she was quiet and kissed her son good-bye.

It was the longest three hours of her life. But then sponsors started texting pictures of Jared having fun and interacting with other classmates. "I hadn't given him credit for the social savviness he has," she said. The dance was a good experience and Jared got a little boost in confidence about handling things on his own, without a backpack full of tips from Mom on how to act.

Hold back instead of dominating—that's what Jan has learned, and it's taken six years since his illness to let him jump out of the nest. She said:

> There is a certain peace that comes in letting go. We shatter peace in trying to control. Things go wrong; hand it over to God. For me, that's the wonderful thing about faith. I'm not just handing my son or his problem over to the air or some concept, but handing him over to his spiritual Father and Creator—and that brings me a lot of peace.

"Did We Forget Something?"

When my neighbor Eddy Helker and I were talking about the process of releasing sons into manhood, he shared this analogy:

> When Evan [his seventeen-year-old] is driving out of the driveway, I may think of things I forgot to tell him. So I run out, ask him to stop the car, and start reeling off twenty different instructions. That's a microcosm of what we do as parents: we want to hold on to our young people because we think they're not prepared. We think there's something we forgot to teach them. Out of fear, we hold back and don't want them to go.

The problem, Eddy says, is we didn't start with the end in view.

As a high school teacher, Eddy has taught hundreds of adolescent and twenty-something guys and has some great insights into what it takes to prepare them for adulthood:[14]

First, think about . . . *I'm going to be releasing my son into manhood. How am I going to pray, prepare, and equip him with what he needs?* These questions are so much better to ponder ahead of time than to get to the end of their teenage years and try to throw everything in.

It helps to picture your son grown and consider what you hope he will be, what goals you have for him, what purpose God has for him. Sometimes our hope, our idealized picture of our adult son is someone who's a successful, ethical businessman, or a super athlete or an achieving academic person with several degrees. Less often is the goal a picture of a man who loves and follows Jesus with all his heart and knows His presence and passes on truth to his children.

Pray and ask God to show you not only what your picture and goal is but what *His purpose is for your son's life.* Then pray and plan: What do I need to train and equip him in so he can be that man?

As you consider your aim for your children, pastor Jim Cymbala provides a good perspective in his book *Fresh Faith*:

> Did you know that parents can feed their children three nutritious meals a day and put the latest $120 sneakers on their feet and still deprive them spiritually? To withhold from children the knowledge of the wonderful and loving God who created them is the worst kind of parenting. They cannot truly live without Jesus, regardless of the top-drawer education they might receive.[15]

If we help them learn two things—loving Christ and His Word, and knowing the presence of the Holy Spirit—our sons will have a strong foundation to build their life on. And what a gift you'll be giving your son to let him launch out into the next chapter of his life with grace and your blessing.

Questions to Ponder, Journal, or Discuss

1. What responsibilities or decisions could you delegate to your son at this phase of development?

2. Think about what you don't need to manage anymore: Is it your son's eating and food choices, appearance and hair color, choice of friends or _____? Make a list.

3. A college boy's mom insists on setting a curfew when he's home for Thanksgiving and coming into her bedroom to check in after he returns each night, with the reason that "I can't sleep when you aren't home." She's been sleeping nightly while he's been on his own for three months on the university campus a few hours away. Why could this scenario and demand cause conflict between mother and son?

4. What is your picture of what your son will be like when he grows up? When you close your eyes and think about him, what comes to your mind's eye?

5. What is your greatest aim or longing for your son and his future? What steps could you take to help him reach that?

14

A Mom Who Pursues a Purposeful Life

Love wholeheartedly, be surprised,
Give thanks and praise—
then you will discover the fullness of your life.

—Unknown

Our children are a huge priority, but we moms shouldn't neglect ourselves. Recently I met Shawn, a mom of two elementary-age children, who shared with me what she does to keep healthy and pursue some of her passions while keeping family at the forefront of her priorities. Besides endeavoring to eat right, she pencils in exercise times on her calendar, even though she has to split the times up and be very flexible.

With a home-based marketing agency, Shawn works when her kids are at school and builds her work projects around their schedules. With these demands, she could be at the computer all day, focusing only on tasks in the job and at home. "But then I'd be spent and miserable, exhausted with no energy for my kids and no fun with my husband." She aims for thirty minutes of exercise a day, scheduling in five minutes of push-ups here and ten minutes there for walking on the treadmill in her home or neighborhood.

Shawn's joy is cooking, and she finds ways to give back to the community by volunteering at the community food bank. Partnering with a chef and nutritionist, she teaches people how to cook and feed their families in a healthy way. She also loves to offer hospitality and cooks for family and friends.

Shawn is pursuing a purposeful life while her children are still at home. Women of this generation, I believe, are better than my generation of mothers at being intentional about scheduling times for renewal, for friendship with other women, and working out—without feeling guilty.

Another mom, Amanda, has at least one girlfriend night out a month, and works out for her own sanity and to recharge her batteries. She works part time as a speech pathologist and believes she's a much better mother when she does things that enrich her life, even with a busy family. It's a good thing dads today tend to be much better than the generation before them at caring for the kids so Mom can have some time off!

Many mothers today connect with other women in monthly book clubs, in MOPS (Mothers of Preschoolers), or homeschool coop groups, Bible studies, prayer groups, or at the gym. How wise they are not to go it alone or be so busy they neglect face-to-face time with friends. There are great benefits to cultivating these connections, because when you cultivate friendships, you enjoy better physical health, have lower stress levels, and even longer lives.

Someday all of our children will leave home to pursue their life journey as an adult or college student, to perhaps marry and start their own families, so it makes sense to begin living a purposeful life *now*. Don't wait until your dear ones are packing the car and waving good-bye to take good care of your health and emotional well-being; don't ignore yourself or your marriage. Begin now to find your spiritual and natural gifts and do something with them, to serve with others in a cause you're passionate about, to be physically active, take care of your soul—and pursue a joyful life. What a great role model you'll be to your sons and daughters.

Is Your Son Back Home?

Perhaps as you read the previous chapter, you thought, *But my son is in his twenties and hasn't left the nest yet.* Or, *He left for a few years and is back. In fact, he likes living here and has no plans to move on.* Although having a son back home can be a blessing—I always love my sons' visits—it can also produce another set of problems or dilemma if it is a long-term stay.

Recently, I read about the word *adultescent* in Sally Koslow's book *Slouching Toward Adulthood: Observations From the Not-So-Empty Nest*. Koslow defines *adultescent* as the growing number of "Americans ages twenty-two to thirty-five caught between adolescence and adulthood in an exploration that seems to go on forever."[1] That exploration may include hopping between jobs without finding one they want to stay with, dating women without wanting to settle down to marry and start a family, or perhaps living in different cities to find where they fit best.

The adultescent condition is portrayed well in the movie *Failure to Launch*, which is about a thirty-five-year-old man who lives in his parents' home and shows no interest in heading into financial and social independence. His parents, particularly his mother, make it so comfortable and easy to stay under their roof that he is unmotivated to take that final step into real, independent adulthood.

Although *Failure to Launch* is fictional, the mom and dad portrayed in the movie are not alone. There are thousands just like them. Koslow observes that one of the reasons for failure to launch is that by working so hard to provide the perfectly problem-free childhood, many parents are unintentionally making it harder for their kids to grow up and leave home. We're not talking about a small number of gals and guys.

In fact, of the college graduates in the class of 2011, 85 percent of them moved back to live with Mom and Dad.[2] One problem with this Boomerang Generation (another name for kids coming back to live with parents after college) is that they experience a lack of motivation in their career, become more passive, and bristle at parents' expectations.

Certainly there are economic factors that play into the situation. The downturn and recession in the last few years has made it harder to get jobs, plus big college loans add to the issue. Yet for many of the parents, it's not what they expected. They thought their child-rearing season was over and they might be enjoying their newfound freedom. For a short time or on a temporary basis, it can be a blessing to have grown children back, especially if they're willing to help pay a percentage of the mortgage or bills and share in housework.

But if you have a son who has come home to roost and is continuing to lounge around, staying out late, sleeping until noon, and showing no signs of growing up, Koslow advises, "People, step away from the adultescents. All together now, let's push back. The best way for a lot of us to show our love would be to learn to un-mother and un-father." While this may sound like harsh advice, it may be the kindest thing we can do

194

if the temporary guest becomes a permanent resident who is mooching and not making an effort to move on.

There are some cultural factors at play here: A new nationally represented survey of over one thousand eighteen-to twenty-nine-year olds showed *they do not feel like adults*. Over 56 percent reported frequent anxiety. Thirty-three percent were depressed and 65 percent said life is full of uncertainty (at least they have discovered that reality). Of these "emerging adults" (another term for this population), some are completely supported financially by Mom and Dad, and a whopping 34 percent say their parents are more involved in their lives than they want them to be. Imagine that!

A twenty-four-year-old I met has been in and out of college, has never held a job, and lives with his mom, playing video games while she works. One engineering major at a state university said his parents let him make his own decisions but are always looking over his shoulder, watching to make sure he doesn't ruin himself.[3] This doesn't fill a young, emerging adult with much confidence.

What a different experience Gene Wilson, a precious woman I know, had a few decades ago when she and her husband kissed their son, Kirk, good-bye at the airport. Kirk got a scholarship to Dartmouth, but since the family didn't have a reliable enough car at the time to drive him all the way from Oklahoma to the New Hampshire campus, the eighteen-year-old flew to White Plains, New York, by himself, and then got a ride to the university. They didn't see him until the end of the school year.

When Kirk arrived at Dartmouth, he called to say that he'd arrived safely and how beautiful the campus was (no cell phones or Internet then). In June, they got to see for themselves when they drove across the country to pick their son up for the summer.

Mom and Dad were both teachers and they sent him what money they could each month, but it wasn't much. Their son was hardworking and independent, and he just managed. He never asked for anything from his parents until the end of his senior year at Dartmouth when he called: "Mother, I'm going to have all these interviews. Do you think I could have a suit?" They went to a local department store to purchase a suit and mailed it to him in time for the interviews. After graduation and work, he attended Harvard for a master's in business and landed a great career at Morgan Stanley, where he worked for twenty-seven years.

There was a time that most adolescents couldn't wait to leave home and embark on their own independent life. And as much as their parents may have missed them, they were glad to see their dear ones develop wings strong enough to fly. There are times when the best thing is for a son to move home from college because of illness, serious depression, or unemployment. But it is temporary, and goals and boundaries are set.

My hope and prayer is that as you prepare your son mentally, spiritually, physically, and practically in ways we've discussed in this book . . . as you become his greatest encourager in all the steps along the way and support his growing up and becoming independent, he will develop the mind-set and confidence he needs *and* be equipped with the character and skills to launch into being a full-fledged adult.

"Mom, Are You Going to Be Okay?"

One thing I've heard over and over from young adults is that when they leave home for the university or a new job across the country or world, they want to know that their mothers are going to be all right without them. They want their moms to take care of themselves because they really love them—and also so they don't have to be anxious about them.

Sons worry about their mothers being lonely or depressed, and especially if there are major health problems. One woman's son worried about her when she was in a hospital because of serious problems caused by her medication. Two little boys I know worry about their mama when she's sick. Another young man saw his single mother drinking too much and was worried about the effects of her increased alcohol consumption.

Our son Justin worried about me when my husband and I had financial and job-related problems. When there was an ongoing crisis, he worried about the strain it put on me and how I had to "double-compensate" (as he called it) to make ends meet. He was plagued by "what ifs," such as, *What if this doesn't get better?*

Chris told me that as an adult he worried about some health problems I was dealing with as well as the same things his brother was concerned about. "But we feel you and Dad are quite the survivors; you're strong, and you've been through a lot but are in a better season. We admire you." Chris is by nature not a worrier, and I certainly don't want to give him or his brother cause to worry.

In fact, I've assured our three grown children that I don't want to ever be a burden on them. Yet I know I can't control how things are going to turn out in the latter part of life.

Even though they said, "Mom, that's morbid," I sat down and told them that I was asking God to let me keep doing three things that started with *s* until He calls me home: *singing* (I sing in the choir at church and love music, love worship, and love participating in this); *swinging* (a tennis racket, that is. I have played since I was fourteen, and play every Friday morning with three tennis friends); and *serving* (in our nonprofit ministry

Redeeming the Family and other ways God calls me). This was a very short conversation; they didn't want to talk about it and changed the subject.

Do we get our wishes or prayers granted regarding these issues? No, certainly not always. Yet God does tell us to, and invites us to, *ask*. We're going to look at four areas that a mom can do something about, in the transitions and changes ahead that will enrich life for you and make you a blessing to your adult son and family:

- Take care of yourself
- Fill your cup with friendship
- Practice gratitude
- Find a new purpose; find your next chapter

Take care of yourself. One of the best things we can do for our grown sons is to keep taking good care of ourselves, starting with putting ourselves on our long to-do list. Your list may include doing many things for a lot of people and taking care of others—but doing something for *you* is absent. If so, put some items on the list that will help you be healthier and more joyful:

- Strength training three times a week
- Walking, biking, or some kind of aerobic exercise you enjoy
- Eating healthy, even if you're only preparing food for two. It's harder if you're cooking for one, but still is an important part of staying well.

Rather than being selfish, taking care of yourself is a gift you give your son so that he will have the emotional and mental energy *he needs* for tackling his job, caring for his wife and children, and other things he'll face in adulthood.

Fill your cup with friendship. Connection with girlfriends is important at every stage of life, but especially when your children are in the adolescent years and start separating from you. Then when our sons and daughters leave the nest, we need close friends we can spend time with and confide in so we can avoid spilling out our problems to our kids. Whether we are single or married, all women need friends. It can be challenging when we work all day and come home exhausted to the demands of a household, caring for aging parents, and other responsibilities. We can get isolated.

In big cities and even spread-out rural areas, many women are lonely and lack time or access to make deep connections with other women. It's not just using artificial, electronic means like Facebook or Twitter that fills our cup. It's actually spending time with others. By tying ourselves to our smartphone and iPad screens, substituting that for face-to-face time together, we're actually crowding out real time with friends and family. "Friending" on Facebook is no substitute for real, in-person connection. We need the encouragement that friends can offer, and when we're with them it lifts our spirits as well.

Having girlfriends to talk with is a great stress reliever, as is walking, serving, or exercising together. Burdens and worries are lifted when we pray with our friends. I've found the old saying is true that friendship divides burdens and multiplies joys, and am truly grateful for the friends I have had during our kids' college and adult years. I've gained perspective and courage from my friends to carry on in the best of times and worst of times. I've been deeply appreciative of their prayers, and the fun we have as well.

Three dear friends—Cynthia, Corrie, and Susan—and I go out to lunch four times a year to celebrate our birthdays, and we all look forward to these times of fellowship at a tearoom or restaurant. It's not the only time we see one another, but we have those dates on the calendar, not to be crowded out.

A few summers ago, I traveled to Maine with my two best and longest friends, Mary and Ann, to celebrate our forty-year friendship—what a memorable time it was! I love my tennis friends: Laura, Debbie, and Patty. We've played on a public court for over fourteen years, wind or sun, hot or cold. I am grateful for my writer friends; we may be in different parts of the country but it's a treat when we get together or talk on the phone. Weekly I meet in a renewal group with friends Sheron, Missy, Denise, Teresa, Sissy, Jean, Linli, and Gene. What a blessing friends are.

Are you having a bad day? Call a friend. Do you need advice or counsel on a dilemma you're facing? Have coffee with a friend and discuss the issue. We're better off physically, mentally, emotionally, and spiritually when we don't live our lives all alone. And our sons will applaud these relationships, because then we're happier and more fulfilled.

Practice gratitude. You can be a powerful influence and role model to your adult children if you practice gratitude. Yes, there are trials and adversities of many kinds. But each day brings us blessings and gifts, and gratitude helps us loosen the ribbons so we can enjoy them.

"Focus on what God can do, what he is doing, and what you're thankful for," suggests Catherine Hart Weber, psychologist and author of *Flourish* (Bethany House, 2010). Your son doesn't need to keep hearing what's wrong with him. He wants to hear what is *right* with him and what you appreciate and love. You may only see small glimpses of good or mature qualities. Sometimes you may be thinking, *Who has taken over my son's body? He's changed a lot, and I don't know if I like the changes.* If so, take a small notebook when you're descending into disappointment and write down grateful thoughts about him, positive things you see, what is unique about your boy.

Being grateful for who our sons are becoming and what they do, later giving thanks for their families and all the ways they bless us, brings a sweeter relationship. When we feel and express gratefulness for someone in our lives, our gratitude can change a life and definitely pleases God. A mom, mother-in-law, or grandma who is grateful can better connect with the Lord and others.

Find a new purpose. After their sons leave home, moms need to find a new purpose and passion for their lives, in other words, your next chapter. It's never too late to start a new ministry or mission to help others. I've been inspired by the fruitful lives of women I know who've touched the lives of people and made a difference in the world.

Several years ago, I became concerned when I read newspaper articles about the devastating effects on children in our state whose mothers are in prison. Since Oklahoma has the highest incarceration rate of women in the U.S., over 26,000 children have either one or both parents behind bars.

I created a curriculum, "Parenting Beyond Bars," and began going behind the razor wire to teach mothers how to encourage, pray for, and reconnect with their children. After teaching over 380 mothers at our maximum-security women's prison, I discovered a great need: Most of the children never got to see their moms, never got to look into their eyes and see how much they love them.

A few friends and I formed a nonprofit organization called Redeeming the Family with a mission to support these kids who are the most at-risk, disadvantaged children in our state. We brought the Messages Project to Oklahoma, and with an outstanding board of directors, God's guidance, donations, volunteers, and a lot of work, we launched the Oklahoma Messages Project in 2011.

Teams of volunteers go with us to do the Messages Project at men's and women's prisons before Christmas, Mother's Day, and Father's Day. We coach the parents in how to share a loving, positive message with their children. We bring new, donated books for the parents to read on camera. Then after the day of filming, we send the DVDs and books to the children so they can read along and know they're loved and not forgotten, hear how proud their parents are of them, and how much they're missed. While the kids have bedtime stories with their parents via video every night, it also decreases their anxiety to see their parents are safe. We've sent out messages to over two thousand children and found they have a very positive impact on the kids, families, and the parents behind bars; it begins healing in the family and delivers a powerful message of God's love.

You can probably tell I'm passionate about this mission and perhaps understand why I hope to keep doing it as long as God allows. A side benefit is that it gives me very little time to feel sad that my children have left and have busy families of their own. In fact, it turns out some of our grown-up kids and families have helped with the Messages Project team, and I'm really thankful for that. Daughter-in-law Tiffany volunteers as a parent coach, and daughter Alison is one of our videographers, as is my husband. Justin has donated to the project, and all three of our adult children and daughter-in-law Maggie are supportive and surprised that in the sixth decade of their mom's life, I'm the director of a new organization I never dreamed of leading, in prisons where I'd never been, and in a ministry where, as my nephew Raymond says, "my deepest gladness and journey intersect with great need."

I believe God has surprises for us in every decade of our lives as we look to Him and follow Him. I've seen over and over that the Lord has real and important purposes for each one of us not only when our children are at home in the active-parenting years but also when those years have come to a close.

Part of His wonderful blessings to us in the decades following active motherhood is getting to be a grandma. You can look forward to that season! My six grandchildren call me "Nandy," and they light up Holmes's and my life. Oh, how grateful I am for each precious grandchild and every opportunity I am given to spend time with them or cheer at their athletic and dance events.

Let me encourage you, dear reader, in whatever season you are to choose *joy*. Find joy in small things: the cool breeze, the flowers in your garden, sunrises and sunsets. Find joy in giving your life away and in offering a cup of cold water to someone who needs it. Instead of being so absorbed with "me, myself, and I" that you forget there's a world of hurt out there, use the skills and resources God has entrusted to you for a great cause. It will bring you and others so much joy. And remember, "The joy of the Lord is your strength" (Nehemiah 8:10), so don't let circumstances or difficulties rob you of His joy.

There is a wonderful future and hope for you and your children and grandchildren, now and in the years ahead! I pray for God's richest and sweetest blessings for you in every part of the journey.

I challenge you, Mom:

- Give your son the gift of knowing that your identity isn't wrapped up in him. Rather than "I need him to make me look good," recognize your boy's uniqueness and bring out his best.

- Build foundations of faith in your son's life through Scripture and prayer, nurturing his early spiritual life but not controlling or micromanaging it when he reaches adolescence.

- Prepare your son to be a confident young man so at the appropriate time he'll be ready to take on adult responsibilities—not to hold him back by doing things for him that he can do for himself or enabling him.

- Build your son's character and help him become a hard worker, a student who manages his schoolwork and completes chores at home, and takes responsibility for poor choices when he makes them.

- Take care of yourself so you will be healthy and vibrant while your kids are at home and after they leave. Your son won't have to spend his emotional resources worrying about you because you aren't taking care of yourself. He needs to handle his own challenges, carry on with his own life and job, and tend to his own family.

- Put yourself on your to-do list.

- Live a purposeful life—finding things you're passionate about and doing them.

- Pursue the things you always wanted to do just for fun, whether it's compiling your family history, saving for and taking a trip to a foreign country, developing a new career, learning to scuba dive or speak another language, or writing that book you've always had an idea for.

- Make a bucket list and start checking items off as you accomplish them.

- Avoid wanting your son to keep needing you, because it can lead to clipping his wings and making him feel guilty for leaving.

- Allow your son to do life his way after he leaves the nest, knowing that you believe in him. If he sees the world differently than you, and you don't agree with his choices, accept him, love him, and pray for him—and never give up on God's best for him.

- Dream a new dream, something that brings joy just thinking of it. When you develop a new interest or work toward your dream, it fills part of the void of no longer being the caretaker to children. To your adult son, it can also make you a more interesting person to interact with and talk to.

- Find someone you can serve or help who could never pay you back. When you miss having a child at home, mentor or tutor a child in the community who has no one to encourage his education or life.

- Changes are inevitable, but in the midst of them, hope in God and trust Him for all the plans He has for you and your son.

Questions to Ponder, Journal, or Discuss

1. Who are your closest friends? Ask God to open your eyes and heart to a new person to invite into your circle of friendship.

2. What have you always wanted to do but haven't yet pursued?

3. What's the most challenging part of taking care of yourself physically, spiritually, or in other ways?

4. Has your son ever worried about you? What was his concern?

5. What brings you the greatest joy?

6. What ministries, causes, or mission are you involved in—or would like to be?

Recommended Books

Ross Campbell, *How to Really Love Your Child*

____, *How to Really Love Your Teenager*

____, *How to Really Love Your Angry Child*

Dana S. Chisholm, *Single Moms Raising Sons: Preparing Boys to Be Men When There's No Man Around*

Cyndi Curry, *Keeping Your Kids Afloat When It Feels Like You're Sinking*

Stephen James and David Thomas, *Wild Things: The Art of Nurturing Boys*

Rick Johnson, *That's My Son: How Moms Can Influence Boys to Become Men of Character*

Dan Kindlon and Michael Thompson, *Raising Cain: Protecting the Emotional Life of Boys*

Donald Miller and John MacMurray, *To Own a Dragon: Reflections on Growing Up Without a Father*

Art Murphy, *The Faith of a Child: A Step-by-Step Guide to Salvation for Your Child*

William Pollack, *Real Boys: Rescuing Our Sons From the Myths of Boyhood*

Michael Ross and Susie Shellenberger, *What Your Son Isn't Telling You: Unlocking the Secret World of Teen Boys*

John Townsend, *Boundaries With Kids*

____, *Boundaries With Teens*

Notes

Chapter 1: Mothers and Sons

1. William Pollack, *Real Boys: Rescuing Our Sons from the Myths of Boyhood* (New York: Henry Holt, 1998), 57.

2. John and Helen Burns, *What Dads Need to Know About Daughters/What Moms Need to Know About Sons* (New York: Howard Books, 2007), 48.

3. Elizabeth A. Carlson, "A Prospective Longitudinal Study of Attachment Disorganization/Disorientation," *Child Development*, 69:4 (1998), 1107–1128.

4. "What Are Little Boys Made Of?" attributed to English poet Robert Southey (1774–1843).

5. Pollack, *Real Boys*, 111.

6. Burns and Burns, *What Dads Need to Know About Daughters/What Moms Need to Know About Sons*, 4.

Chapter 2: A Mom Who Encourages

1. Several years ago I had the opportunity to interview Dr. Carol Dweck, professor of psychology, who with a team of researchers at Columbia University did the first research on intelligence versus effort-praising. For more about this study, which involved over 400 fifth graders, see Gary Hopkins, *Education World*, 2005, www.educationworld.com/a_issues /chat/chat010.shtml. Now a professor at Stanford University, Dr. Dweck

is the author of *Mindset: The New Psychology of Success* (New York: Random House, 2006).

2. My thanks to Ken Wilgus, PhD, for his helpful consulting and insights on adolescent boys for this chapter.

3. Appreciation and thanks to Alison Plum, one of the most encouraging mothers I know, for sharing her experiences with her sons for this and other chapters.

4. Dan Kindlon and Michael Thompson, *Raising Cain: Protecting the Emotional Lives of Boys* (New York: Ballantine, 1999), 257.

5. Patrick Morley, *What Husbands Wish Their Wives Knew About Men* (Grand Rapids, MI: Zondervan, 1998), 11, 34–36.

Chapter 3: A Mom Who Builds Confidence in Her Son

1. *The Great Adventure: A Daily Devotional Journal* (Uhrichsville, OH: Barbour Publishing, 1999), i.

2. Jane Healy, *Your Child's Growing Mind* (New York: Doubleday, 1987), 86.

3. My sincere thanks to Ruthie Hast, MEd LPC, counseling therapist at Encore Life Skills, for her willingness to answer my questions and share her experiences.

4. Chick Moorman, *Parent Talk* (New York: Touchstone, 2003), 20–21.

5. Leslie Vernick, *The Emotionally Destructive Relationship* (Eugene, OR: Harvest House, 2007).

6. From "Say It's Okay to Fail," *Woman's World*, August 27, 2012, 45.

7. Stephen James and David Thomas, *Wild Things: The Art of Nurturing Boys* (Carol Stream, IL: Tyndale, 2009), 184.

8. Thanks and appreciation to Kendra Smiley for sharing her story with me. She is the author of *Live Free: Eliminate the If Onlys and What Ifs of Life* (Chicago: Moody Publishers, 2012). www.kendrasmiley.com.

Chapter 4: A Mom Who Overcomes Her Fears

1. Neil T. Anderson and Rich Miller, *Freedom From Fear* (Eugene, OR: Harvest House Publishers, 1999), 25.

2. http://www.justmommies.com/articles/new-moms-fears.shtml.

3. Lawrence O. Richards, *Expository Dictionary of Bible Words* (Grand Rapids, MI: Zondervan, 1985), 58.

4. Anderson and Miller, *Freedom From Fear*, 25.

Chapter 5: A Mom Who Prays for Her Son

1. Jennifer Kennedy Dean, *Legacy of Prayer: A Spiritual Trust Fund for the Generations* (Birmingham, AL: New Hope Publishers, 2002), 18.

2. Fern Nichols, *Every Child Needs a Praying Mom* (Grand Rapids, MI: Zondervan, 2003), 16.

3. E. M. Bounds, *The Possibilities of Prayer* (New Kensington, PA: Whitaker House, 1994), 9.

4. Dean, *Legacy of Prayer*, 14.

5. Oswald Chambers, *My Utmost for His Highest*, updated edition, James Reimann, ed., (Uhrichsville, OH: Barbour, 1992), 178.

6. Richards, *Expository Dictionary of Bible Words*, 524.

7. F. B. Meyer, *The Secret of Guidance* (Chicago: Moody Publishers, 1997 edition), 78–79.

8. Nichols, *Every Child Needs a Praying Mom*, 20.

Chapter 6: A Mom Who Listens and Communicates

1. Burns and Burns, *What Dads Need to Know About Daughters/What Moms Need to Know About Sons*, 72.

2. Story adapted from my book *The Mom You're Meant to Be* (Carol Stream, IL: Tyndale House, 2003), 44.

3. Moorman, *Parent Talk*, xvii.

4. Kindlon and Thompson, *Raising Cain*, 247.

5. Ibid., 248–249.

6. Pollack, *Real Boys,* 110.

7. My thanks again to psychologist and family counselor Ken Wilgus, PhD, for sharing his wisdom on communicating with adolescents and how to avoid control battles.

8. Michael Gurian, *The Purpose of Boys* (San Francisco: Jossey-Bass, 2010), 33.

Chapter 7: A Mom Who Stays Connected

1. Rhonda Ross, *Southlake Style* (Southlake, TX, June 8, 2012), 45. http://southlakestyle.com/2012/06/08/Seventh-Heaven.

2. Pollack, *Real Boys*, 82.

3. From an interview with Mrs. Edith Schaeffer.

4. Kindlon and Thompson, *Raising Cain*, 243.

5. Pollack, *Real Boys*, 100.

Chapter 8: A Mom Who Understands Her Son's Unique Personality

1. Burns and Burns, *What Dads Need to Know About Daughters/What Moms Need to Know About Sons*, 4.

2. Stella Chess and Alexander Thomas, *Know Your Child*, second edition (New York: Jason Aaronson Publishers, 1996), 63. Used with authors' permission. Another good resource for parents who want to learn more is Stella Chess and Alexander Thomas, *Goodness of Fit: Clinical Applications From Infancy Through Adult Life* (Philadelphia: Taylor & Francis, 1999).

3. Chess and Thomas, *Know Your Child*, 30.

4. Kindlon and Thompson, *Raising Cain*, 125.

5. Healy, *Your Child's Growing Mind*, 10.

6. Harville Hendrix and Helen Hunt, *Giving the Love That Heals: A Guide for Parents* (New York: Simon & Schuster, 1997), 12.

7. Daniel Goleman, *Emotional Intelligence* (New York: Bantam Publishing, 1995), 195.

8. Chess and Thomas, *Know Your Child*, 30.

9. Marcelene Cox, quoted in Edythe Draper, ed., *Draper's Book of Quotations for the Christian World* (Wheaton, IL: Tyndale, 1992), 227.

10. Psalm 139:13–16 and Jeremiah 29:11.

11. David and Jan Stoop, *The Complete Parenting Book* (Grand Rapids, MI: Revell, 2004), 203.

Chapter 9: A Mom Who Helps Her Son Shine in School and Beyond

1. Miles McPherson, *The Power of Believing in Your Child* (Minneapolis, MN: Bethany House, 1998), 198.

2. To read Dr. Benjamin Carson's autobiography (which is also terrific to read together with your son because of the positive role model Dr. Carson is), see *Gifted Hands: The Ben Carson Story* (Grand Rapids, MI: Zondervan, 1990).

3. James and Thomas, *Wild Things*, 141–142.

4. Ibid., 132.

5. Kindlon and Thompson, *Raising Cain*, 23–24.

6. Ibid.

7. Quoted in Michael Gurian, *The Minds of Boys: Saving Our Sons From Falling Behind in School and Life* (San Francisco: Jossey-Bass, 2005), 219.

8. Kindlon and Thompson, *Raising Cain*, 30–31.

9. Brian's story adapted from my book written with Louise Tucker Jones, *Extraordinary Kids* (Colorado Springs: Focus on the Family, 1998), 103–105.

Chapter 10: A Mom Who Develops Her Son's Character

1. Thomas Lickona, PhD, quoted in "Raising a Moral Child," (*Child Magazine*, December/January 1993), 130.
2. Ibid.
3. Dr. Flip Flippen, family and adolescent counselor, Bryan, Texas, quoted from a personal interview.
4. Lynda Hunter Bjorklund, EdD, quoted in David and Jan Stoop, *The Complete Parenting Book* (Grand Rapids, MI: Revell, 2004), 257, 259.

Chapter 11: A Mom Who Helps Her Son Manage His Emotions

1. James and Thomas, *Wild Things*, 238.
2. Ibid.
3. Pollack, *Real Boys*, 41, 81. Pollack is referencing a Rutgers University study that shows how moms of young boys and young girls treat them differently, how they soothe baby girls more when they have negative emotions, and how this begins a shame-based process that discounts and eventually leads to shutting down the emotions of boys.
4. My appreciation to Michelle Garrett, family counselor, for her insightful portraits of her sons' emotional styles and effective ways to help them manage their feelings.
5. My heartfelt thanks to Tiffany Fuller, my daughter-in-law, a loving mom and a wise family counselor, for consulting and giving ideas on this chapter and points on communicating with boys.
6. Cyndi Lamb Curry, *Keeping Your Kids Afloat When It Feels Like You're Sinking* (Ann Arbor, MI: Vine Books, 2002). Available at amazon.com.
7. Pollack, *Real Boys*, 112.

Chapter 12: A Mom Who Nurtures Her Son's Faith

1. Leslie Leyland Fields, "The Myth of the Perfect Parent," *Christianity Today* (January 2010), 27. www.christianitytoday.com/ct/2010/january/12.22.html.
2. From an interview with Art Murphy, used with permission. To learn more about this helpful approach to faith development, see his book *The*

Faith of a Child: A Step-by-Step Guide to Salvation for Your Child (Moody Publishers, 2000) or visit www.arrowministries.com.

3. Anne Graham Lotz, in Introduction to *Daily Light for Every Day.* First published in Great Britain in 1794 by Samuel Bagster; revised edition (Nashville: J. Countryman, 1998), v.

4. Fields, "The Myth of the Perfect Parent," *Christianity Today*, 27.

5. Joe White, *Sticking With Your Teen* (Carol Stream, IL: Tyndale, 2006), ix.

6. Fields, "The Myth of the Perfect Parent," 27.

7. Anne Graham Lotz edition (1998) of Samuel Bagster's *Daily Light for Every Day* (Nashville: J. Countryman).

8. Dr. Arch Hart and Dr. Catherine Hart Weber, *Is Your Teen Stressed or Depressed?* (Nashville: Thomas Nelson, 2004), 223–234.

9. My grateful appreciation to Dr. Ken Wilgus for his wisdom and advice about adolescents and their faith.

10. John Henry Jowett quoted in *Streams in the Desert*, by L. B. Cowman, edited by James Reimann (Grand Rapids, MI: Zondervan, 1997), 289.

Chapter 13: A Mom Who Releases Her Son to Manhood

1. James and Thomas, *Wild Things*, 298.

2. Ibid., 236.

3. Ibid., 241.

4. Walter Wangerin, *Ragman and Other Cries of Faith* (New York: HarperCollins, 2004), 128.

5. Ibid., 130.

6. James and Thomas, *Wild Things*, 234.

7. Kathleen Volk Miller, "Helicopter Parenting in the College Years," *Family Circle*, September, 2012, http://www.familycircle.com/teen/parenting/communicating/helicopter-parenting-in-the-college-years/.

8. Ibid.

9. McPherson, *The Power of Believing in Your Child*, 21.

10. Ken Wilgus, *Fwd* (a publication of Christ Church Plano, Texas), 2004, 1–2.

11. Poem "If" by Rudyard Kipling, from *Internet Modern Sourcebook*, www.fordham.edu/halsall/mod/modsbook.html. Public domain.

12. Lynda Hunter Bjorklund, "Teaching Values and Building Character in Your Child," in David and Jan Stoop, *The Complete Parenting Book: Practical Help From Leading Experts*, 262.

13. From an interview with Michelle Garrett, counselor and mother of two boys. Used by permission.

14. My appreciation to Eddy Helker for sharing in an interview his insights on building foundations of truth and releasing our children.

15. Jim Cymbala, *Fresh Faith: What Happens When Real Faith Ignites God's People* (Grand Rapids, MI: Zondervan, 1999), 100.

Chapter 14: A Mom Who Pursues a Purposeful Life

1. Sally Koslow, *Slouching Toward Adulthood* (New York: Viking Penguin, 2012), 18.

2. Ibid., 18–19.

3. From an article by Sharon Jayson, "Many 'Emerging Adults' 18–29 Are Not There Yet," *USA Today*, July 30, 2012, http://usatoday30.usatoday .com/news/health/wellness/story/2012-07-30/Emerging-adults-18-29-still -attached-to-parents/56575404/1.

Acknowledgments

I want to acknowledge the terrific people who helped make *What a Son Needs From His Mom* possible.

A sincere, grateful thank-you to:

Holmes Fuller, my immensely loving and patient husband who cheered and prayed throughout the writing process *and* helped me with final edits.

Sons Justin and Chris for allowing me to write about your growing up and for your contributions.

Ali Plum and Tiffany Fuller, my favorite mothers of boys on the planet, for your contributions! How you love your kids is an inspiration.

Maggie Fuller for lots of encouragement—and to our six grandchildren: Caitlin, Caleb, Noah, Luke, Josephine, and Lucy for bringing me so much joy.

The wonderful prayer team who undergirded this project with their prayers so faithfully: Betsy West, Sheron Davis, Elaine Shaw, Janet Page, Peggy Stewart, Glenna Miller, Jill Miller, Linda McClain, Amy Andrews, and my dear Renewal Group friends at FPC: Missy, Sissy, Jean, Denise, Gene, Teresa, Jayne, and Linli.

Greg and Becky Johnson of WordServe Literary Group, agent and dear friends, for your insights on raising boys.

Dr. Ken Wilgus, for consulting editorially, for contributions and insights on raising adolescent boys.

Ruthie Hast, for candidly sharing her counseling skills, contributions, and experience raising two sons.

Jennifer Kennedy Dean, Leslie Vernick, Kendra Smiley, Michelle Garrett, and Eddy Helker for sharing their experiences and expertise on raising boys.

For all those who were kind enough to let me interview you and share your story, I truly appreciate you.

Jeff Braun at Bethany House for being a great editor and having a heart for this book.

The editorial and marketing team at Bethany House Publishers in Minnesota. Thank you for all you've done to bring *What a Son Needs From His Mom* to print so it can encourage mothers and improve their relationship with their boys!

Cheri Fuller is a gifted speaker and award-winning author of more than forty books, including the bestselling *When Mothers Pray, Raising Motivated Kids*, and *A Busy Woman's Guide to Prayer*. Her books have been translated into many languages, and her speaking ministry has provided encouragement to people throughout the United States and abroad. A former Oklahoma Mother of the Year, Cheri has been a frequent guest on national TV and radio programs. Her articles on family, spiritual growth, relationships, and prayer have appeared in *Family Circle, Focus on the Family, Guideposts*, and many other publications.

Cheri holds a master's degree in English literature and is executive director of the nonprofit organization Redeeming the Family. She and her husband, Holmes, live in Oklahoma and have three grown children and six wonderful grandchildren.

Cheri's books, Bible studies, and other resources can be found at www.cherifuller.com, along with information on her speaking topics and how to schedule Cheri for events. To find out more about the ministry, visit www.redeemingthefamily.org.

More Insight for Christian Parents

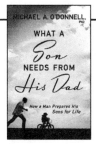
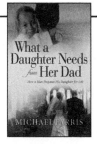
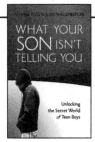